THE WRATH
OF IVAR

*The Viking Blood and
Blade Saga (Book 2)*

Peter Gibbons

Cover design by: Erelis Design
Library of Congress Control Number: 2018675309
Printed in the United States of America

For Mary and Peter.

My mother said to me
That they would buy for me
A ship and lovely oars
To go away with Vikings,
Standing in the stern,
Steering the glorious ship,
Then putting into ports,
Killing a man or two.

EGIL SKALLAGRIMSSON, 10TH CENTURY
VKING WAR POET

ONE

866 AD.

Hundr stared down the long deck of the warship Seaworm and twenty pairs of hard killers' eyes stared back at him. He had brought these warriors to the mouth of a wide, silted river on the coast of Frankia to hunt and kill. Most were veterans of the war in Northumbria, where the sons of Ragnar Lothbrok fought to control Saxon England. Hundr's thoughts slipped to that Saxon land, a short voyage across the Frankish sea, but the memories were too painful, so he banished them from his mind to concentrate on the battle at hand.

Their minds must be keen, and their actions clear if they were to overcome their dangerous prey. The Seaworm lay in wait, sitting shallow in the river water, dragon-headed prow snarling out into the estuary. Hundr and the crew of the Seaworm waited, tucked away from sight of the river's bends, for fellow Viking raiders. Vicious and merciless warriors trained in warfare from the time they could stand. The Seaworm waited in a hidden inlet on a wide river to catch the Sea Wolves returning from their inland raids. Crews of hungry Vikings used rivers like Roman roads, sailing deep inland hunting for silver and slaves. Hundr and his crew of fighters planned to ambush and slaughter another crew of the most brutal fighters in the world, men just like them. Their prey would be fat with plunder and weighed down with silver. Hundr wanted to take it all from them. He wanted to strike with his sword and hear their screams; he wanted to feel the battle joy coursing through his veins. Most of all, however, he just wanted to hurt someone, for someone else to feel pain like he did, and distract his mind from its suffocating cloy of betrayal and suffering.

The Seaworm crew sat at their oars, gripping the smooth timber shafts with white knuckles. Each man had their eyes fixed upon Hundr, waiting for his order to row and launch into the attack. The crew licked their lips and shuffled, shifting their weight and unable to keep still as they waited for the order which must come soon. Hundr rubbed at the dark pit of his dead eye, which itched constantly. It had been a year since Hakon Ivarsson, son of Ivar the Boneless, had cut the eye from his skull with a red-hot knife. Hakon had died screaming when Hundr snatched his life away with Hakon's own sword. That blade sat belted at Hundr's hip. Soulstealer was its name, and he put his hand on her cool iron pommel for battle luck.

"Shouldn't be long now," said Einar Rosti, Einar the Brawler, leaning on the ship's dragon prow and peering downriver. The dragon gave the Seaworm her name, the fire-breathing giant worm of nightmares. Einar had been Hundr's Jarl, his Lord, before they had fought Hakon. The Seaworm belonged to Einar, and Einar had taken Hundr in when he had nothing. Hundr had begged him for a berth upon his warship at a dank and miserable port in the Jutland peninsula. In those days, Einar was sworn to Ivar the Boneless and served him for many years as a Sea Jarl and war captain before Ivar and his son Hakon betrayed, humiliated, and dismissed him. They left Einar with nothing, no future, and nothing to show for his years of service but his life. The Seaworm belonged to Einar, but Hundr was the leader of the crew.

"I'm going over first," Hundr growled, and Einar nodded. Hundr craved battle. He hungered to lose himself in its mad fury, where he would either kill or be killed himself. Only in those moments, where blades flew and blood flowed, was his mind clear. No images of the war in Northumbria hurting his brain, no thoughts of her, his lost love. He wanted, and needed to go first so he could cut, slash and kill and dampen his own pain in the suffering of others.

"There," said Einar, pointing downriver and then wincing as he clutched at his stomach. It was only a year since Ivar the Boneless had plunged his blade deep inside Einar's guts, and Hundr knew it was a gift from Odin that Einar had survived that terrible wound.

Hundr followed Einar's finger, and sure enough, a long sleek Viking drakkar warship poked its beast-headed prow around a bend in the meandering river. Murmurs rolled down the Seaworms' deck, and Hundr heard the clicking and scraping of weapons loosened in scabbards, the clank of helmets on the hull where men lifted them, preparing for the fight to come.

"Wait," Hundr said, and the ship went quiet.

Einar grinned and drew his axe from the loop at his belt. Hundr thought his friend looked gaunt; his face, which was usually an implacable slab of rock, looked hollow at the cheeks and his skin pale. The ravages of Ivar's wound still taking their toll.

4

"We fight for ourselves now. We serve no one. Anything we take is ours. A man must be the master of his own destiny if he is to be truly free," said Einar. It was the promise they had made to each other as they left England. They would make their own future and never again live at another's whim.

Since sailing away from Northumbria, they had become pirates. A lone ship preying on other Sea Wolves. They could do as they wished, and they had gathered much silver. The men were content, and Hundr supposed that was enough. For now.

The oars of the approaching longship dipped into the river's glassy surface, and Hundr heard the splash as the ship surged forward, slicing through the water like a knife.

"Now. Go," said Hundr.

Einar turned and repeated the order, and the Seaworm crew grunted. They dipped their oars and pulled. That first pull was the backbreaker, the huge heave to get the ship moving. Hundr felt the surge under his feet as the Seaworm lurched forward.

"Faster, pull, pull," Hundr turned and saw gritted teeth and red faces as the men leant into the stroke. Then another stroke. Now the ship wasn't lurching; she was racing. Racing forwards to intercept her prey. Three more strokes, and they were in the river proper, heading into the path of the approaching longship. If they kept on this trajectory, they would smash into the hull of the approaching ship, but that collision would damage the Seaworm as much as it would the other. Hundr waited for a few more heartbeats, one more long stroke.

"Now, bank now!" he shouted. Ragnhild, the Valkyrie warrior, nodded back from the steerboard at the rear of the Seaworm. She grinned across her scarred face and leant on the tiller.

Hundr heard shouts of alarm erupting from the enemy ship. Those men pointed at the Seaworm and looked to their Lord for a command. But it was too late. The Seaworm's oars came up with a grunt at the effort. Ragnhild steered the ship into a sharp turn, and the Seaworm came about just as her bow reached within a stone's throw of the enemy vessel. Hundr saw the surprise on a bearded face across the water, mouth dropping open as he realised what was about to happen.

The Seaworm came around in a shallow arc until she was alongside the enemy ship. Hundr felt the jolt as the impact came, and he braced himself against the prow. Heat rose from his belly, and he allowed himself a smile as the Seaworm's curved prow crunched across the line of enemy oars. Hundr gripped the hilt of his sword and held it tight. He watched as the broken line of oars in the enemy ship snapped viciously. The force of the Seaworm racing across the oar blades in the water caused the handles of those oars to snap forwards into the oarsmen at their benches, Hundr winced at a high-pitched scream as one such oar handle crushed a man's ribcage like an overripe fruit.

"Kill them, kill them now. Take everything from them. Their lives and their silver are ours!" Hundr bellowed and launched himself across the gap between the ships. For a moment, his heart stopped as he thought he would fall short, but then relief came as his feet landed on the timber deck of the enemy ship. Bearded warriors all around him now, snarling and shouting. A boot connected with his back, and Hundr sighed as the cloak of battle calm descended. He whipped Soulstealer free from her scabbard and slashed it at a gap-toothed face. Blood splashed across the deck in thick gobbets like jewels, and Hundr barged a warrior out of the way and whipped a knife free from his belt to plunge its blade into the chest of the warrior who had kicked him. A blade came towards his chest, but Hundr batted it aside with Soulstealer's hilt and bellowed with joy as he head-butted a red-bearded warrior full in the face and dragged his dagger backhanded across that man's throat.

"Odin!" came a shout from behind.

Hundr turned and grinned as Ragnhild leapt onto the enemy ship and lay about her with her axe, shrieking like a demon. It was over then in a few heartbeats, the Seaworm crew swarmed the enemy, cutting and slashing at the Sea Wolves until they were dead or knelt in the bilge. A gap appeared at the stern of the ship where an enormous man stood with an axe in each hand, challenging his enemies to fight him one against one. Hundr stepped forward, wanting to fight the giant. The killing had stopped but hadn't yet sated his thirst for blood. He was too late. Ragnhild already accepted the single combat, and the Valkyrie warrior keened her high-pitched war cry and launched herself at the big man. The gigantic man was stripped to the waist, and his torso rippled with muscle, but Ragnhild moved with extraordinary speed and skill: she danced around the giant cutting at his arms and legs, whilst her enemy slashed wildly at spaces she had occupied a fraction earlier. In a blur of flashing axe blades, the big man dropped to his knees with Ragnhild's axe buried in his forehead. She looked to the heavens and sang a prayer to Odin, then, after wrenching her blade free, she dipped her hand in the blood of her fallen foe and wiped it across her face. Ragnhild cried out again to Odin and kicked the big man's corpse into the river.

The ship was theirs now, all resistance crushed in the time it would take a man to eat his breakfast. The Seaworm crew whooped for joy and searched the ship for treasure and plunder. Hundr sat back on a rowing bench and sighed. The fight had finished too quickly. The battle joy had been fleeting and had now subsided, leaving him with the familiar hollow cavern in his heart. He heard a squeal behind him and turned to see Guthmund, one of the newer Seaworm crew, pull a woman up by the hair from where she hid beneath a bench, caked in mud, and her blonde hair matted and filthy. They had bound her at wrist and ankle, and she sobbed wide-eyed in Guthmund's grip. Hundr closed his eyes tightly as a memory of his own time as a captive flashed before his eyes. He remembered himself dragged behind a horse for miles, falling in and out of consciousness, and then tied to a post where his tormentor cut at his chest with a blade, sheeting his torso in blood.

"Leave her," Hundr said, snapping his eyes open.

"What? Let's take the bitch, give her to the lads,"

said Guthmund, leering, showing brown teeth in his grizzled beard.

"I said leave her. Put her down." Hundr rose from the bench and fixed Guthmund with his one eye. The warrior let the prisoner go, and she scuttled back into her hiding place. "No one is to harm that woman. Drop their prisoners over the side. They can swim to shore."

Hundr picked his way down the ship, over bodies of fallen enemies and shards of broken oars. Three surviving warriors crouched beneath the ship's mast, where Einar spoke to them, brandishing his axe. Einar turned and nodded as he saw Hundr approach.

"A chest of silver and some slaves. Not bad," said Einar.

"I let the slaves go. Who were they?" asked Hundr, nodding to the cowering warriors.

"Raiders, Danes," Einar shrugged. "They say there is an army of Vikings upriver."

Hundr peered around Einar's shoulder at the three men. One wore a Brynjar mail coat, which meant he was a warrior of note. Like a sword, a coat of mail was rare and expensive, and only Lords or warriors with reputation could afford one and be able to stop others taking it from them.

"An army, you say?" Hundr said to the warrior in mail.

The warrior was middle-aged, and his hair was receding across his skull, making his forehead shine in the midday sun. He licked his lips and looked into Hundr's eye.

"There's an army, led by famous warriors. I'll tell you all about it if you cut me loose. Let me join your crew, Lord."

Hundr punched the warrior in the face and slammed his head back against the mast.

"Strip his mail, cut his throat and throw him in the river," said Hundr. Einar grabbed the man by his hair and dragged him away. The warrior whimpered and so Einar kicked him in the belly. Hundr turned to the two remaining survivors.

"Now. Tell me about this army."

The two survivors sang like birds, and they told a tale of Vikings fighting deep in Frankia alongside a Frankish Lord in his war against a rival. Hundr probed them, wanting to learn as much detail as possible.

Since leaving Northumbria on that rain-soaked day a year past, since the day he had fought and beaten Ivar the Boneless, Hundr and the crew had sailed aimlessly up and down the coasts of Saxon and Frankish Kingdoms. They had raided here and there but with no real purpose or plan. The Seaworm was short of crew upon leaving Northumbria, and so they had taken on new crewmen at a port in Northern Frankia. Guthmund and his men were a band of masterless men, a mixture of Danes and Norsemen, looking for a Lord to serve. Hundr and Einar had taken them on to bring the Seaworm up to her full strength and allow for faster sailing and more effective raiding. Having no purpose other than raiding here and there had allowed Hundr to wallow in his pain. He knew he had allowed the darkness of his betrayal by those he loved and the physical pain he had endured to overwhelm him.

The prospect of an army and a war to fight caught Hundr's attention. A war would allow him to immerse himself in that conflict. He would have a purpose again. When he was younger, all Hundr thought about was reputation, how he had to leave his home in the East and prove himself as a warrior. He had fled and joined Einar's crew and fought for the sons of Ragnar Lothbrok in the war against King Aelle of Northumbria. Hundr dared to say he had a reputation now. He had fought Ivar the Boneless, the Champion of the North. Hundr had taken one of Ivar's swords that day, along with Soulstealer. He had two fine swords to show for all that suffering. Another war meant battle and purpose, but the decision was not his alone to make.

Hundr leapt back aboard the Seaworm and called to Einar and Ragnhild to join him. The three stood close to the steerboard and watched as the crew loaded the ship with the fruits of their attack.

"Good haul this time," said Ragnhild. Their previous raid on a small fishing hamlet had yielded nothing but dried fish and stale bread.

"Aye. Still not enough silver though," said Einar.

Einar and what remained of his old crew had fixed on a plan to gather as much silver as possible. He had been serving Ivar the Boneless on a promise of becoming a landed Jarl in the newly conquered Northumbrian lands, but that promise had turned to ash on the fire of Hakon Ivarsson's treachery. Einar and his men were past middle age, and so they had looked forward to settling down and becoming farmers and starting families. A warrior cannot keep on fighting forever. He either finds his place in Valhalla, or he settles down. Hundr owed Einar his life. Einar and Ragnhild had stormed a hilltop fortress against impossible odds to rescue Hundr from Hakon, and Hundr would do anything he could to repay them for that. So, he had sworn to help

Einar find enough silver to buy a swathe of land somewhere where he and his men could settle.

"At this rate, it will take many years to get enough silver," said Hundr.

"How much is enough?" said Ragnhild.

"Four times what we have now, maybe more," said Einar with a shrug.

"The prisoners say there is an army upriver, a Viking army," said Hundr. He glanced at Ragnhild and Einar. Ragnhild scratched her chin, but Einar frowned, creasing his hard slab face.

"And?"

"War means silver," said Hundr.

Einar shook his head.

"Surely you have not forgotten already what it means to serve another? We swore never to serve another Lord; we are the Lords now."

"I haven't forgotten," said Hundr, tapping his finger on his missing eye and ravaged face.

"Who leads this army?" said Ragnhild.

"A man called Haesten. A man with reputation, they say."

"I have heard of him," said Ragnhild. "He sailed far to the south, to the land of the Blamen whose skins are burned black by the sun."

14

"I have heard of him," said Einar. "He has a reputation alright, for trickery and battle luck."

"So, he sounds like an interesting man. We don't need to swear an oath to him, Einar."

"He sailed south with Bjorn Ironside. Son of Ragnar Lothbrok, and brother of Ivar the Boneless."

The sound of that name, Ivar the Boneless, spoken aloud made Hundr's guts twist. He spat over the side, watching the crew secure the chest of silver in the bilge.

"Take their weapons, everything of value," Hundr shouted to the men. Weapons could be sold and traded just like silver. There were two slaves, both women, and Hundr wasn't sorry he had let them swim away. It had cost him some grumbling and sideways glances from Guthmund and the newer crew, but he had been close to a slave himself and so wouldn't see those women continue to be ripped from their homes and families and forced into continued servitude upon his ship.

They poled away from the defeated ship and rowed back upriver towards the sea and away from Haesten's army. Hundr didn't know in which direction to sail. He wanted to sail upriver and join with Haesten. He wanted to fight and forget about Ivar and Northumbria. Hundr knew Ragnhild wanted that fight. She was born for battle and had trained her whole life for it. But he owed Einar his life and wouldn't go against his friend. So, they sailed again in search of silver for Einar's dream.

TWO

The river opened up into a wide estuary at the end of its long, meandering journey to the sea. Its banks changed from forest and reed-filled greenery to hillocks of dark tidal silt dotted here and there with small wooded islands. Hundr felt a cool breeze tickle the small hairs on the back of his neck. Soon, they would unfurl the sail and give the crew a rest from their oars. Hundr and Einar had come to an informal and unspoken arrangement. Einar was in command of the ship, and Hundr was in command when it came to battle. Hundr wasn't sure himself how or why that had taken shape. Einar held a well-known reputation for ferocity as the winner of many bouts of single combat, but since Northumbria he had become withdrawn from such matters, and the crew had leaned towards Hundr for orders and leadership whenever blades were drawn. He had a talent for death if nothing else, but in exchange for that talent, he worried the Norns, the three witches who spin the threads of men's lives at the foot of the world, had cursed him with ill luck.

The river was peaceful, undisturbed by the gentle passing of the Seaworm. He felt a scratch on his elbow where a blade had caught him in the fight upriver. He watched two ducks as the ship glided past, wondering if they were a pair and were there ducklings nearby. That thought gave his mind a pathway to shift to thoughts of Saoirse, that unwelcome train of thought which plagued him constantly. When he closed his eyes, he could see her long, gentle face with its wash of freckles as though she were there, standing before him. He loved her now as he had loved her from the moment he had rescued her from a Saxon ambush deep in the Northumbrian woodland. But she had left him. She had watched Hundr kill her husband, Hakon Ivarsson, and then she had gone with Hakon's father, Ivar the Boneless, to become his wife, leaving Hundr alone. Deep down, he knew she had done it to protect her people in Ireland, to maintain the peace between her father's warriors and Ivar's warriors who occupied her homeland. But the pain of it still burned like a knife in his chest. She was an Irish Princess with responsibilities to her kin and people, and he had been a fool to think they could ever escape and build a life together somewhere in peace.

Hundr leant over the sheer strake of the ship, between the shields which hung from its edge and all along the ship facing out towards the shore. He dipped his fingers into the cool river water and allowed them to drag there. The water was refreshing and cool on his fingertips. He wondered where she was now, his Irish Princess. Was she living back in Ireland, or in a fortress with Ivar somewhere. Maybe she was already heavy with child. That thought sank him even lower. Hundr pulled his hand back in and wiped the cool water across his face. It had not been Saoirse alone who had left him. Hundr thought of his friend Sten Slegyya, Sten Sledgehammer, who also had betrayed him.

"A piece of hack silver for them," said a voice, snapping Hundr from his painful memories.

He looked up to see Ragnhild staring down at him. She clapped him on the shoulder and sat on an empty bench opposite him. Ragnhild was his friend. They had each saved one another's life, and he trusted her like a sister.

"For what?"

"Your thoughts,"

He nodded and looked across at the ever-widening estuary. They would be at sea soon.

"Wondering where to go next," he said.

"North?"

"Still thinking about Upsala?"

"I will have to return at some point."

"If they will take you back."

She nodded solemnly. Ragnhild, Hildr, and Hrist, the three female warriors amongst the crew, had left their order of Valkyrie warrior women to join Einar and Sten Slegyya in their rescue of Hundr. She had been with the order her entire life. It was all she had ever known. She was a sworn servant and warrior priestess of Odin All father and fought in his name and under the orders of the high priest of her order's home in Upsala.

"What we did that day pleased Odin. Few fought against many, and we sent many skilled warriors to Valhalla."

It was true. That assault on Hakon's fortress had been a fierce battle indeed. They named the Valkyrie for those howling servants of Odin who fly down from the heavens to collect the souls of warriors who die in glorious combat and who carry those souls to fill Odin's great hall, Valhalla, where they feast and fight for eternity. The occupants of that hall will fight for Odin at the end of days, Ragnarök, where he will fight against Loki and his army of monsters.

"So, you think High Priest Vattnar will take you back?"

"He might," she shrugged.

"Einar needs more silver."

"How much is more?" she asked, which was a good question. All Einar wanted was some land for himself and his old crew. They wanted to settle down, find wives, and have children.

"I can't see him becoming a farmer," Hundr said, and Ragnhild laughed.

"He doesn't want to be a farmer, he just thinks he does. Einar and his men are destined for Valhalla, to die with blades in their hands. He'd be bored within a month. He just hasn't recovered yet."

"His wound has healed well, thanks to you, Hildr, and Hrist."

"Not the blade wound," she said and tapped a finger to her temple. "The wound in his mind. Einar was and is a great warrior with reputation. He suffered that terrible wound that does not kill, the one all warriors fear. Can he still throw himself amidst the blades and fury of battle when he knows the pain and horror of that wound, the fear of dying in his bed without his blade and being denied a place in Valhalla?"

"Maybe he will settle down then. Find a wife," said Hundr.

"He's no more a farmer than you or I."

Hundr laughed because she was right. It felt good to laugh. He felt lighter for it. She looked at him, her one eye blazing from deep within her scarred face. She, too, had lost an eye. They shared that wound, and its pain, the knowledge of that suffering brought them closer together.

"Let's go North. We can find some rich pickings on the way, more silver for Einar if that's what he wants."

Hundr nodded. It was as good a plan as any, he supposed. She smiled a gap-toothed grin and clapped him on the shoulder again. Hundr rose from the bench and stretched his back. He looked back along the ship's long hull and over the heads of the warriors who rowed at a gentle pace. Einar stood, as he always did, at the tiller on the steerboard platform. Hundr still thought of him as Jarl Einar. A Jarl was a Lord who owned land and men under the rule of a King. Einar had been a sea Jarl. He had no land but commanded the

Seaworm and her crew under Ivar's rule. That had all changed in the maelstrom of Hakon Ivarsson's cunning. Einar looked out onto the water beyond, his grey eyes scanning the horizon and the wind ruffling his long hair. He looked happy, Hundr thought. Northmen loved ships and sailing, and Einar was no different. Hundr chuckled again, thinking of Einar at the plough or milking a cow.

"Sails!" came a shout from behind.

Hundr turned to look. It was Bush, one of Einar's surviving original crewmen, so named because an arrow had once shot him whilst shitting behind some bushes, much to the crew's amusement.

"There, see?" Bush said, pointing North.

Hundr focused his eye, and there indeed were two ships heading in their direction under sail.

"Can you make out the sails?" Hundr asked. Northmen decorated their sails with emblems to mark them out, often fierce beasts to cast fear into the hearts of their enemies.

"Not yet," said Bush.

Hundr glanced back to Einar. He shook his head and shrugged.

"Half pace, lads," Einar said to the crew. They

23

barked a clipped shout to confirm they understood the order, and the ship slowed its pace.

Hundr kept his eyes on the ships, who clearly headed for the river the Seaworm now departed.

"They're drakkars, warships," said Bush. "Sitting too shallow to be knarr traders."

Northmen, sea wolves just like us. He looked back at Einar again. If the ships attacked, they couldn't fight off two crews.

"Raven banner, the sails carry the Raven," said Bush, and he glanced at Hundr.

Hundr felt the eyes of the entire crew on his back, and his face flushed. The Raven was the banner of the sons of Ragnar Lothbrok, that dead Viking hero and champion who had spawned a brood of kings and famous warriors. Chief amongst them Ivar the Boneless. *He has come for me.* Hundr swallowed the rising heat in his throat and did his best to maintain a look of calm. He stalked towards Einar at the tiller, avoiding the eyes of the crew who stared as he passed.

"Ivar," said Einar, as Hundr approached.

"What do we do? We can't fight them," said Hundr softly so that the men wouldn't hear.

"We can't. If he is in the Windspear, which he

probably is, then he's faster than us. So we can't outrun him. You killed his son, and you beat him and took his sword. He could never accept that. We knew he would come for you."

Suddenly, the scabbard strapped to Hundr's back felt heavy. He kept it there, Ivar's sword. It was a beautiful thing, forged by the finest smiths in Frankia with dragon breath in its blade. It felt like a boulder on his back now, almost rattling as it felt its master closing in. Ivar had two such swords, Hugin and Munin, thought and memory, named for the Ravens who sat at Odin's shoulders. Hundr had taken Munin, memory, from Ivar the day he had beaten him, man against man on a rain-soaked Northumbrian jetty. The same jetty where Hundr had killed Ivar's son, Hakon, moments earlier. He had their swords, Soulstealer and Munin, and he had Ivar's hatred. Ivar was the champion of all the Northmen, the greatest of all Viking warriors. He was fast and vicious, and Hundr had beaten him. With his monstrous pride and reputation, Ivar would not rest until Hundr was dead.

"Go back to the river," said Hundr.

"They'll trap us there."

"I have an idea."

Einar gave the order, and the crew quickened

the pace. A few long pulls at the oar to quicken her, and then one bank of oars raised high above the waterline as the opposite bank bit hard into the water's glassy surface. Einar pushed hard on the tiller, and the Seaworm came around. She came about in a wide arc, and all the time the Ivar's ships grew closer, chasing them down. Hundr's belly felt soured and hollow as he watched them closing in. He was certain he saw a green cape flapping in the wind against the lead ship's prow beast, Ivar's cloak.

The Seaworm raced back up the estuary, and the men grunted as they pulled hard, fighting against the river's flow. Hundr glanced back. The Raven was clear now on the lead ship's sailcloth, huge, black and terrifying.

"What's the plan, then? They'll be upon us soon," said Einar.

"Wait until we get past that island," Hundr said, pointing ahead at a long narrow strip of forest growing in the centre of the river and splitting in two.

Hundr could hear the warriors in the chasing ships bellowing their war cries. The Seaworm crew sweated and grunted to quicken their pace, but the Boneless' ships were longer with more oars. It wouldn't be long now before they were overrun. The Seaworm came within ten strokes

26

of the island.

"Steer into the shallows there and drop me off," said Hundr. Einar looked at him wide-eyed, but Hundr held up a hand to stop his friend from interrupting. "Drop me in the shallows, and I'll wade to the top of a sandbank. You turn around the island and head back to sea. Ivar won't follow, he'll come after me."

"Are you mad?"

"There's no other way, and you know it. Ivar is bloody mad for my head. Take the ship and return in one week. I'll be here. A week, Einar."

"Or you'll be bloody dead."

"In which case, I'll save a place for you in Valhalla."

Einar shook his head and grimaced. He leant on the tiller, and the ship veered towards a sandbank.

"What are you doing?" called Ragnhild from the prow.

Hundr raised a hand to her and leapt overboard.

THREE

Hundr sucked in deep breaths to fill his lungs. The chill water knocked the wind out of him as he plunged into its murky depths. It had been deeper than he expected, reaching to his chest so that when he landed, he couldn't find his feet, and Hundr had felt a moment of panic. His Brynjar mail coat and weapons would drag him down into the Sea God Njorth's embrace if the water was too deep, but he had found his feet and now waded, gasping for the shore.

Einar stuck to the plan, and Hundr glanced over his shoulder to watch the ship bank around the island where she would race back to the open sea. Hundr emerged dripping from the water, mail and leather lining heavy and soaked, but his boots caught in the heavy sandbanks and he fell. Rising, he turned to see where the Windspear was. Ivar's two ships were running parallel to him, and Hundr must get Ivar's attention if he was going to lure him away from the Seaworm. The plan had come to him quickly. Now stood there alone, soaking wet, teeth chattering from the freezing river water, he wasn't so sure. The Seaworm would be safe, he hoped, but he now had to goad Ivar ashore and then escape his fury. Ivar would kill Hundr if he caught him, and it wouldn't be a quick death. Ivar was renowned for torture and for making a show of fallen foes.

Hundr drew Soulstealer from her fleece-lined scabbard at his waist and Ivar's old blade, Munin, from his back. Hundr held the blades out wide and waved them towards the Windspear. River water stung his dead eye, and it seeped from the empty socket and down his cheek.

"Ivar the Boneless. I killed your piece of shit son, and I beat you, man to man. I am the champion of the North. Come and fight me."

Hundr heard a roar erupt from the decks of Ivar's two ships. They backed oars and came to rest directly in front of where Hundr stood on the riverbank. Ivar himself appeared in the stern of the Windspear, his green cloak marking him out amongst the browns and greys of his men in their leather and wool. *Are you there, Sten?* Hundr scanned across the gathered warriors but couldn't find his old friend. Sten was an enormous man, probably the biggest man Hundr had ever seen, and easy to spot in a crowd.

"I see you, dog," Ivar roared across the water. "You Rus turd. I'll have your head, dog."

Hundr laughed loudly, deliberately loud, just to annoy Ivar even more. His name, Hundr, meant dog. Einar Rosti's crew had awarded him that name when he had been reluctant to give them his real name, his Rus name. Now, Hundr knew, men referred to him as the man with the dog's name.

"Come and die, Ivar, you shit stinking coward."

There was a commotion aboard the Windspear as Ivar roared with rage and made to jump over the side. His men held him back, and he was lucky. The Windspear was a larger ship than the Seaworm, and sat lower in the water, which stopped her from getting close to the shallows. So, any warrior jumping into the river water fully armed and wearing heavy mail would never surface again. Ivar barked an order, and two warriors jumped over the side whilst Ivar removed his weapons and mail coat.

The two warriors who leapt into the river wore only light leather armour, and so, after splashing into the cold water, they swam slowly towards Hundr. They swam slowly because they tried to swim whilst holding axes above the waterline.

Hundr waited and watched. He laughed again and beckoned Ivar to follow his men ashore. But the Boneless did not follow, he waited. Hundr strolled down to the water's edge, resting his two blades, one on each shoulder. The warriors drew close now, red-faced and gasping for air as they found their feet and stood in the slippery river mud. The water there reached their waists, and they came on with plodding steps, panting and laboured from the swim. Hundr glanced to his right and saw that the Seaworm was pounding her oars hard upstream towards the whale-road. They were free, and his plan had worked. That part of it, at least.

One of the two approaching warriors lost his footing in the slick river bottom, and he lurched forward, scrambling on his hands in the mud. He was a young man, younger than Hundr, who thought he had seen nineteen summers. Hundr sprang forward, and Soulstealer snaked out, straight and hard, like a dragon's tongue, and its tip punched through the young warrior's gullet. His eyes went wide, and his mouth fell open as thick blood flooded his chest. Hundr brought Munin down overhand to slash her blade across the warrior's face. The blow sent him toppling sideways into the water. The other warrior shouted in defiance at Hundr, and he tried to be fast. He tried to lunge forwards and whip his axe blade at Hundr's face, but he misjudged the depth of the water. It slowed his lunge, and the axe blade flew short. This second warrior was short and swarthy and had a tattoo of a swirling demon on his cheek. Horror twisted the man's face into a grimace as he realised his attack had failed. He closed his eyes tight against the pain which must follow. Hundr punished that mistake. He spun, bringing Soulstealer around in a long wide arc, and her blade cut through the swarthy warrior's neck like a scythe through dry summer sheaves.

There was more shouting now from Ivar's ships. Hundr grinned and raised his blades in salute. Spears flew from the second ship, which had edged closer whilst Hundr killed Ivar's men. He had to skip backwards up the sandbank as three spears slammed into the water where he had stood moments earlier. Hundr dropped Soulstealer to the sand and bent to pick up a spent spear. He took a step forwards and launched it towards the Windspear. It fell short, but Hundr hoped he was still annoying Ivar. As the Seaworm raced away into the distance, the Boneless faced a dilemma. Hundr had known Ivar would break off pursuing his friends when he spotted him alone on the shore. But if Ivar himself jumped into the river as his men had done, he surely must suffer the same fate. Hundr would simply cut him down as he tried to leave the water. Ivar could send all his men over the side, and they would overwhelm Hundr. Ivar was not stupid, however, and if Ivar did that, then surely Hundr would run, forcing them to chase him across the fields and forests of Frankia.

"I'm waiting for you, Ivar. Your men died like children. Are you afraid?" Hundr called.

Ivar just smiled at him. The Windspear's warriors dipped her oars again, and she moved slowly ahead, whilst the second ship backed oars and reversed the way she had come, so they would come ashore in front and behind him and try to trap him between both crews. Hundr knew then he had to run. If they caught him, his death would be long and painful. He turned to go, but something on the second ship caught his eye. Hundr stopped and stared at that ship. He was sure he had seen a big man with silver hair stalking the deck. He looked again, but the figure was no longer there. *I hope it's not you, Sten.* Hundr turned and picked up his sword. Then, keeping one blade in each hand, he ran across the sandbank and up onto the shores of Frankia.

The riverbank swept gently from the silt sandbank into an elm and ash forest. Hundr scrambled up a briar-filled ridge, pulling himself up on gnarled exposed roots and ran into the welcome shadows of the wood. He knew that Ivar's warriors would do the same, leaping from the warships onto the shore. Ivar would have offered a reward, an arm ring or some freshly plundered Saxon coin for Hundr's head. That thought made his bowels clench, but it also imbued him with energy to run from their blades. He hopped over a fallen branch and twisted around a thick trunk as he sped through the undergrowth. Hundr hoped Einar, Ragnhild, and the crew were well away by now, sailing on to the safety of the Frankish sea. He was here alone, but there was no time to worry about that now, not when two crews of bloodthirsty Vikings were hunting him.

"I see the bastard, there," a voice came from somewhere in the shadows.

Hundr cursed and pumped his legs harder, ignoring the burning in his thighs and chest. His soaked mail and its leather lining felt like he was carrying a horse. He wasn't even sure if he was still running away from the river. It was hard to tell in the deep forest where everything looked the same. He could easily blunder his way right into Ivar's blades, but he just had to keep on running. It wasn't honourable for a warrior of reputation to flee, to show his back to the enemy, but to stay and fight meant to die.

Something whistled past his ear and slammed into the tree ahead; a goose feather fletched arrow quivered from the force of the impact. *The bastards have bows.* His head shrunk involuntarily into his shoulders at the thought of archers with a bead on his back. Arrows had pierced him before, in a grim fight on a Saxon bridge, and he shuddered at the memory of that pain. Another arrow sped past, wide of him but still ominous. Hundr twisted, mazing his run to throw off the archers. He heard crashing amongst the undergrowth to his left, on the blind side of his dead eye. He couldn't turn to look with his good eye, but he veered in that direction. The archers would be less likely to shoot if their own men were in the line of sight, and he would rather die fighting and go to Valhalla with honour than to be shot in the back.

"Here, here, I have him," came the shout from his left, close now.

Hundr stopped and turned. He dragged Soulstealer from her scabbard and a knife from his belt. A lanky, shaven-headed warrior charged him, only a few steps away. This had to be the shouter, the fastest of his crew, maybe. Hundr saw the joy on the man's face as he thundered towards him. But the warrior had made a mis-

35

take, and it would cost him his life. He had been so quick to get on the chase that he had forgotten to draw his weapon. Hundr grinned at him, and the lanky man's face dropped as he fumbled for the axe at his waist. Too late. He was only two steps away, and his momentum carried him forward into the hard steel of Hundr's weapons. It was too easy to kill the fool. Hundr sidestepped and feinted with the sword, flicking her tip at the last minute, so the man used his own body-weight to kill himself on her long cold blade. Hundr twisted Soulstealer so she wouldn't become stuck in his guts, then pulled her free in a gout of blood. Lanky fell to his knees, and Hundr ran again.

An arrow slammed into a tree beside his head, and he heard feet crashing from the way Lanky had come. So Hundr ran the other way towards the archer. The missiles were coming slowly, so he hoped there was only one. An arrow flashed from behind a tree, and it slammed into his side. The impact spun Hundr around. It was like being kicked by a horse, and he gasped at the pain. He reached for the shaft, arm shaking at what damage he might find. There was no shaft. His mail had turned the arrow point aside. Hundr laughed. *They can't kill me. Odin is protecting me.* The archer showed himself ahead, peeking around a thick tree trunk. Hundr stopped and stood still, holding his bloody sword aloft.

"You can't kill me. Odin protects me. I will kill you all," Hundr shouted. The battle fury flooded over him and he laughed again.

The archer nocked another shaft to his bow, and Hundr noticed movement in the trees behind the bowman. To run now would mean an arrow in his back, so he charged at him. The bow came up, and the archer drew the string back to his ear, but Hundr was within ten paces of him now, and he roared from the pit of his stomach.

"Odin!"

The archer went wide-eyed, and he loosed his missile, but he panicked, and the shaft flew high, whistling above Hundr's head. Hundr closed the gap and whipped Soulstealer around, slashing the archer across the face and feeling the resistance as the tip scraped the man's skull behind his nose. Hundr didn't stop moving. He turned, sprinting away, the crashing of feet and the roaring of his enemies behind him. Alone and pursued by his foes, Hundr dashed through the woodland, branches tearing at his face as he ran deeper into the forest's shadows and away from Ivar's wrath.

FOUR

The Seaworm rose and fell gently in time with the ocean's swell, calm waves lapping rhythmically at her hull. It was a bright and clear night, with a full moon shining huge and bright in the heavens surrounded by a blanket of twinkling stars. Einar looked at the brightest star, the North star, hanging there to show all Vikings the way home. Einar hadn't ever had a home in the traditional sense. Never owned land of his own, born and raised on the estates of the Lords his warrior father served. Einar was married once when he was young, but she had died. To his shame, Einar had never loved that woman. He had fallen into the marriage; it was a mistake. His only love in those days was the sea and reputation.

"The moon is bright," said Hildr, one of Ragnhild's Valkyrie warriors. She sat opposite Einar, where some of them had gathered together to share a pot of ale before bedding down for the night.

"On a night like this, you can see the genuine beauty of the Gods," said Ragnhild.

"We used to have a skilled storyteller on our old crew," said Blink. "Old Thorkild had a head full of stories. Tales of Gods and heroes of old."

"Poor bastard. I hope he's in Valhalla telling stories there," said Bush.

Thorkild sailed with Einar from the time he had first served Ivar many years ago. Thorkild had survived the battle against Hakon and Ivar in Northumbria, but an arrow had shot him through the thigh. The wound had festered, and the old storyteller died a week later, shivering and dribbling shit down himself, no way for a warrior to go.

"That cluster there," said Ragnhild, pointing to a collection of stars above them, "is Aurvandil's toe."

"Aurvendil's toe, surely there isn't a star named after someone's bloody toe?" said Brownlegs, and they all laughed. All but Ragnhild, who laughed rarely.

"Thor carried Aurvendil across the ice waves of the Ellvagar rivers in a basket. Aurvendil's toe froze, and Thor cast it into the sky. There," said Ragnhild, her finger tracing the shape of the toe in the sky, "you can see it."

"I see it," said Blink, slapping Brownlegs on the back.

"I wonder if Hundr is looking upon the same sky somewhere," said Hrist.

Einar looked at her and then out across the black sheet of the sea. It reflected the sky in its darkness, rippling and swaying with the swell. He hoped the lad was alive.

"It was a brave thing, drawing them off like that," said Brownlegs.

"We knew he would come, the Boneless. No way could he let it go," said Bush.

Einar nodded. He knew Ivar better than most men, having served him for so long. Ivar was a generous Lord, a good ring-giver to his men. But he was also viciously violent and unpredictable. He was the greatest and most skilled warrior amongst all Northmen, and any man would fear his wrath.

"What happened between Ivar and Hundr?" said Guthmund. He was one of newer crew members, one of the masterless men they had taken on board to fill out the crew after fleeing Northumbria. Those men sat separate, but close enough to hear their conversation.

"Hundr fought Ivar in single combat, and Hundr beat him. Killed Ivar's son in front of him, too," said Brownlegs.

"He fought Ivar the Boneless and won?" said Hrorik, another of the men with Guthmund. "Surely you don't expect us to believe so tall a tale?"

Bush shot up from his bench and pointed at Hrorik. "He beat him. And done much more besides. Stormed the walls of Yorvik, killed Hakon Ivarsson. Now he's alone, in a land he doesn't know, hunted by two crews worth of killers. You stay quiet. You weren't there."

Einar stood and put a hand on Bush's shoulder and pushed him back to his seat.

"That's enough for tonight. Everyone get some sleep. Tomorrow, let's hope for some wind in the sails," Einar said.

The crew nodded and went to prepare their blankets for the night. He watched as Hrorik and Guthmund whispered together as they moved around the ship. Einar didn't trust the new men. Masterless men were untrusted wherever Northmen sailed. Every man had a Lord. A warrior served his Lord, and his Lord rewarded loyalty with safety, silver, and arm rings if you were lucky. The Seaworm had been short of men. So few survived the fight with Hakon and Ivar, and so they had taken whoever they could find to crew the ship properly.

"I'll take the first watch," Einar said, and went to sit on the steerboard. Ragnhild followed, and Einar welcomed her company.

"He saved our lives back there," said Ragnhild.

"He did, bloody fool."

"Ivar will hunt him."

"He'll never let it go. Ivar won't rest until either he or Hundr are dead. They'll chase him across Frankia if they have to. One week." he said. "Then we're to meet him where we left him."

Ragnhild sat next to Einar and drained her ale.

"So what do we do?" she said.

"Hug the coast, find food and ale. Wait until the seventh day and go back up the river."

"What if Ivar is still there?"

"What can we do? We have to go back for him."

She nodded slowly and looked out across the sea. Einar knew she was thinking the same as he. The Seaworm was under-manned as it was. They barely had enough crew to sail her, never mind fight two larger ships filled with Ivar's killers.

Ragnhild was no coward, and nor was Einar, but to go up against Ivar now was suicide.

"What then?" she said.

"I need more silver if me and the lads are going to settle down."

"How much silver?"

Einar shrugged. He didn't know how much. Einar had never bought land before, nor had he thought seriously about where he would live or who would sell it to him. He could just take it by force, but then he would always await a revenge attack, looking over his shoulder for someone to take his land from him.

"Do you know much about farming?" Ragnhild asked.

"No. But I can't keep fighting forever."

"You can look for the glorious death in battle, earn your place in Valhalla."

"I daresay I've earned my place already. I want some peace now. Ivar promised me land before all that madness happened, before Hakon happened. The lads want wives and children. We need to leave something in this world, not just take from it."

Ragnhild nodded slowly, but Einar wasn't sure she understood. He wanted a wife, maybe even children, and he knew Bush and Blink and the others did too. But she was right. Einar knew precious little about farming. He could use slaves for that. He just wanted a kind woman, a good hall, and a warm fire. Ragnhild was devoted to the service of Odin. All she saw in her future was a glorious death, her only ambition to take her place among the Einherjar; Odin's warriors in Valhalla.

"I need to go North, Einar," Ragnhild said, fixing him with her one eye. "Me, Hildr, and Hrist must get back to the Valkyrie and return to our order."

"They might not take you back."

Ragnhild had left her Odin-sworn order of female warriors, the Valkyrie, to join the rescue of Hundr in Northumbria. She and a handful of her fellow Valkyrie had ridden with Einar and Sten against the orders of her High Priest, Vattnar.

"I have to try," she said, "but first we get Hundr back."

"First, we get him back. Then we take you North. Maybe Hundr will want to go East, back to his homeland. We have never spoken of it, but you remember what he said after the fight with Ivar."

"I remember. That he was the bastard son of a Rus Prince."

"Maybe we'll go East. Maybe that's where we'll

find enough silver."

Ragnhild walked across the hull to join Hildr and Hrist for the night, and Einar remained where he was to take his watch. He hoped Hundr was alive, that he hadn't been prideful and tried to fight Ivar and his men. Einar wondered if Sten Slegyya was on board the Windspear or Ivar's other ship. The old warrior had surprised them all in his betrayal. He was like a father to Hundr. Hundr had been through so much in his young life, he couldn't have seen over twenty summers and already had a reputation as the man who had beaten the champion of the North, the man with the dog's name. Einar remembered the day he first met Hundr, at a fish-stinking trading port in the Jutland peninsula. The boy had asked for a berth, looking like a beggar with no silver and no weapons. But Einar had seen something in the lad that day, something in his eyes, a strength or maybe a destiny. He hoped Ivar had not caught him. Ivar was as famed for his spectacles of torture as he was for his battle prowess. Only a year ago, Ivar had cut the blood eagle on King Aelle of Northumbria's back, and that surely was a fate worse than death.

****

Hundr clenched his teeth together to stop them

from chattering. His whole body shook, but his jaws involuntary shivering was driving him mad. He lay half-submerged in a freezing brook, a shallow stream which wound its way babbling through the Frankish woodland. It was not freshwater, it stank of decay and rot, but he lay in it and was glad of it.

Ivar's men had chased him all day and into the night. His legs throbbed from running, and his chest heaved, gasping for air as he had spotted the hiding place. A bent and twisted tree reached across a gap in the undergrowth, and at the base of that sprawling black trunk was the gently babbling brook where he now lay. It wound its way around the trees and ferns, but the brook cut under that black tree in a sharp turn. Its waters had washed away the soil below the trunk and exposed dark and tangled roots clogged with half-rotted leaves. Hundr lay there now, the stinking water freezing his limbs, but the cover of the roots hid him from his enemies. Hundr had pushed himself as far into the roots as he could. He'd smeared his face and hands with the filthy mud from below the water's surface and lay there clinging to the roots, like a night demon waiting for Ivar's men to pass.

Warriors marched past, first one way and then another. Hundr lay in the filthy water and lost all sense of time. It could have been an hour or an entire day he lay there hiding. Eventually, the sound of their footsteps dwindled. He assumed it had been too dark for them to continue the hunt. Ivar would be furious, and that thought warmed Hundr. It warmed him and helped him ignore the cold. If Ivar caught him, Hundr knew his death would last for days. He would suffer under Ivar's knife, victim to one of the Boneless' elaborate tortures, and would then die without a blade in his hand. He would be forced then to wander the hel of eternity outside Valhalla with the nithing wraiths who had not earned a glorious death in battle.

Hundr thought he had seen Sten onboard Ivar's second ship. It could have been him, or just another big, hulking old warrior which was unlikely, but possible. In the year since Sten's betrayal, Hundr had flitted between furious hatred of his old friend and sadness that their friendship was lost. Sten made his bargain with Ivar to protect Hundr, Einar, and Ragnhild. Hundr knew that, but it didn't make it any easier to swallow. Dwelling on Sten's betrayal led Hundr's mind to Saoirse again. Every time he closed his eyes, her face was there. He wondered what she was doing. Was she happy? Did she miss him as he did her? But for now, he had to think on more pressing matters. In the morning, there was no doubt Ivar would continue the hunt. Hundr's only hope was to keep pushing inland and drive Ivar away from his ships. If he could stay alive long enough, then Ivar would be forced to return to his boats or risk losing them. So, Hundr was alone. Lying in a stinking ditch and smeared with mud. He had to run for his life and then make it back to the river in seven days, where he hoped Einar and Ragnhild would return for him. Otherwise, he was alone and lost in a foreign land.

FIVE

Hundr lay awake all night, huddled beneath the cloying damp of the twisted roots. His stomach sour with hunger, his tongue thick from thirst. He had drunk nothing since jumping from the Seaworm, not having any time to secure any supplies in the heat of Ivar's pursuit. The brook's turgid water surrounded him, but Hundr didn't dare drink from it or risk becoming gut sick. Sleep was impossible. The forest at night was alive with rustling, snuffling, and the cries of unknown beasts hidden by the blackness. From his hiding place, he couldn't see anything around him. The rustling could be a harmless animal foraging for food in the safety of the night, or it could be Ivar's warriors searching for him quietly, sneaking to his hiding spot to slip an icy blade into his body. Worse still, it could be a night demon, a forest walker, or night creeper searching for prey in the forests grim depths. Any slight level of visibility the moon could bring to the dense forest was obliterated by the night canopy, leaving Hundr in complete and utter darkness. Unseen creatures with tiny tickling legs crawled over his skin, making him jerk and bat them away, and the cold, wet mud and water seeped into his clothes and bones, but he was still alive.

Time became fluid that night. Hundr had no sense of how long he huddled beneath the gnarled tree and its grasping roots. He found himself engaged in a battle, not with blades and bows, but a battle with his own mind. Any broken twig or rustled bracken around him brought visions of Ivar. Ivar's odd eyes, one blue as the sea on a summer morning and one deep brown like the pelt of a bear, peering at Hundr from that unnervingly handsome face. Hundr shrugged off those visions, and more time crawled by. Visions of Ivar, however, became replaced by equally unwelcome memories.

His dead eye ached with the cold, and Hundr vividly recalled the lightning-white pain of the hot knife as Hakon Ivarsson dragged its blade down his face and burned out the jelly of his eye. Hundr had wept under that knife, and he wept again in the darkness of the Frankish forest. Saoirse, too, tormented him. The vision of her beautiful smiling face as they marched together across the wilds of Northumbria lifted Hundr's spirits, only to have them torn asunder as he remembered the calm and unflinching look on her face when she stepped over the dead body of her husband to leave Hundr and join Ivar. Worst of all, Sten came to him that night.

Sten came in that ethereal twilight realm between half-sleep and wakefulness, which blurs dreams and reality. The hulking old warrior Sten Slegyya, known wherever Vikings sailed, champion of Ragnar Lothbrok, first over the wall at the siege of Paris, killer of Ketil the Black, and Jarl Thorgrim Redbeard. Sten came to plague Hundr's mind, first as a friend advising and helping him, almost like the father Hundr had never had, then as the betrayer. Sten the Betrayer was no longer smiling. In this mind-wrenching night vision, he was the tattooed wielder of Warbringer, the huge double-bladed war axe Sten had taken from Magnus No Ear during the assault on Hakon Ivarsson's fortress. The last person to visit Hundr's thoughts during that long night was his mother.

She came to him dressed in her fur-tipped finery. He remembered the sweet smell of her hair and the softness of those furs where they brushed against his skin. In his mind's eye, she told him she was proud of him and that his father would be proud of him. That last part of her appearance confirmed that it was just Hundr's mind playing tricks on him in the darkness. His mother had died in his Eastern home years earlier, and his father had never even acknowledged Hundr as his son. His father had other sons born to recognised and honoured wives, not concubines from the North like his mother. Those sons would be full Rus princes by now, Hundr assumed, whilst they had forced him to flee his home and make his own way in the cold harshness of the world.

The wall of darkness eventually lifted. Shafts of sickly yellow light penetrated the leaves and branches, greeted by the grateful calls of birds in the treetops. Hundr assumed that Ivar's men had broken off their hunt once night fell, likely retreating to the safety of their ships for the night. There was no doubt in his mind that Ivar would resume the hunt as soon as light enabled the search.

This was the second day since he had jumped from the Seaworm, and Hundr trusted Einar to bring the Seaworm back up the river in five days' time. All Hundr had to do was stay alive for those five days, which was easier said than done with two full crews baying for his blood. Hundr put his hands into the filth of the brook's bed, feeling the slimy thickness squelch through his fingers. He pushed a knee out and tried to drag himself from beneath the roots and flinched from pain in his side. In the flight through the forest, his mail had stopped an arrow from piercing his skin, but the force of the impact left heavy bruising and stiffness. Hundr crawled from under the protection the soil ledge had provided and rose to his feet. He stretched his back and groaned, his head and throat throbbing from thirst.

Soon, Ivar's warriors would come for him, and Hundr knew they would organise their search today. He assumed those Norse, Danish, and Irish warriors would make a long line on the river's edge and then march through the forest. They would look for any sign of Hundr's passing, and there would be no escape or hiding from them this time. Nightfall had saved his life yesterday, but today he had to put some distance between himself and Ivar.

Hundr pulled himself out of the brook, using a broad branch for support. Around the base of the tree from which that branch grew was a collection of mushrooms and strange branch-like yellow fungus. Hundr's stomach growled, and for a moment he considered plucking the mushrooms and eating them to kill his hunger, but he knew little of forest craft and did not know the difference between the mushrooms which were good for eating, which were good for entering the mind-bending spirit world, and which would make a man sick. He left the mushrooms untouched and marched against the babbling flow of the brook. It was difficult to get a sense of direction in the forest, and Hundr knew he had to head away from the river where Ivar lay in wait. Hundr thought the brook must move towards that river. It would start somewhere inland, and, like all streams and waterways, it would wind its way to join a river, and ultimately the sea beyond.

His trews were soaked wet, and his boots filled with silt and muck from his night in hiding. His hair, hands, and face caked with mud. He had smeared that mud on himself to cover his skin and blend in with the darkness. Hundr thought he looked like a woodland demon, a dark and earthy wraith equipped with fine war mail and two expensive swords.

The forest was now alive with the sounds of birds in the treetops flitting from branch to branch and calling to one another in the morning light. Walking warmed Hundr, but his clothes became crusty and stiff as the dank wetness dried in. Hundr continued along the brook's meandering path, and behind a collection of low bushes pitted with bright red berries, the brook widened into a pond. The water there looked and smelled fresher, and so Hundr knelt and drank deeply. The cool water slipped down his neck in a refreshing rush. He gulped it down and sighed happily as it lifted the fatigue from his limbs. He washed his face and hair and scrubbed the filth from his mail and scabbards. Hundr looked like a warrior again, and he pushed on, continuing to follow the flow of the widening brook.

The morning drew on, and the density of the forest reduced. Hundr had heard no sign that

Ivar's warriors were close. He cautiously approached the thinning tree line, all too aware that he was in a foreign land, filled with a people he knew little about. Hundr had never travelled to Frankia. He knew only that its King was Charles the Bald, the grandson of the famous Frankish warrior King Charles the Great. Hundr heard the Franks were a warlike people and rich like the Saxons. Men rich in silver, and green, fruitful lands. The Franks were also rich in the worship of their Christ God, which meant large minsters and churches just like Northumbria, with fat Priests dripping in gold and silver. Northmen raided Frankia just as regularly as they did the Saxon kingdoms of England. Viking Warships, with their shallow draughts, sailed easily up the many rivers along the Frankish coast to plunder and ravage the fertile countryside.

Hundr reached the edge of the treeline, and his growling stomach somersaulted as a swathe of patchwork fields filled with swaying golden crops unfolded before him. Where the forest ended, rich farmland began. Hundr leaned against a moss-covered trunk and watched for movement in the fields, but all seemed quiet.

Across the first field was a collection of barns and a timber dwelling a little smaller than a Northman's hall but still large enough to house a Lord and some retainers. Hundr patted his growling belly and daydreamed of the food likely stored in those barns. He waited five more heartbeats to spot any sign of people across the field, but saw none. Hundr didn't want to charge into the farm searching for food and be set upon by the Lord and his men. He had Ivar's warriors behind him and the possibility of Frankish blades before him. He decided it was worth the risk to get some food, and so, Hundr strode on through the waist-high crops, the ears of wheat and barley tickling his upturned palms as he walked.

Hundr reached the end of the crop fields and pushed open a small door on rusted hinges to enter the first barn. A horse whinnied across from him where it nodded in a stable. Fresh hay littered the floor of the barn, and the building was busy with scythes, sacks, harnesses, and other such farming equipment. Hundr searched amongst the nooks and crannies for food, anything to fill his belly. Behind a wall decorated with chisels and mallets hung two hams. Two large, glorious haunches gripped by hooks and dangling from the rafters. Hundr allowed himself a chuckle as he drew a knife from his belt and cut a fat slice of meat from the closest haunch. It was drying out and so had lost most of its juices, but the meat was soft and luxurious. Hundr groaned as the taste flooded his senses. He devoured that piece and cut more slices, stuffing them into a sack he found in the corner of the barn.

The stabled horse was huge and powerful. She was chestnut with a white burst on her forehead, and she nuzzled into Hundr's touch as he stroked her powerful neck. She was no warhorse, and Hundr guessed they used her mainly to pull a plough or some other form of heavy lifting. But she would speed him away from Ivar and his warriors. A horse blanket lay draped over the side of the stable, and Hundr threw it over her back. He looked for a bridle or saddle but could find none. Suddenly, the door of the barn opened with a creak, and two men tramped through. They wore heavy boots and tunics smeared with the dirt and sweat of honest work. The two men were of a similar size and had red-cheeked, ruddy faces. One of those men looked up and met Hundr's gaze. His mouth fell open, and he grabbed the arm of the other.

Hundr felt heat rise in his chest, and his hand fell instinctively to the pommel of Soulstealer. They babbled something which Hundr couldn't understand, so he drew the blade a handbreadth from her scabbard. That was enough of a warning. The two men bundled back through the doorway, shouting the alarm. Hundr cursed, turned back to the horse, and she looked at him through the corner of her eye, the whites there large and suspicious. Hundr leant in and kissed her neck. *You must carry me away, old girl, carry me to safety.* He heard a commotion outside the barn, more shouting and feet pounding on the hard-packed earth. Hundr opened the stable stall and led the mare out gently. He grabbed a fistful of her soft mane and launched himself up onto her back, only just able to throw his right leg over her wide back. He patted her neck to calm her, the tug on her mane having caused her to bob her head and paw her hoof. Hundr tucked the sack of ham under his arm and dug his heels into the horse. She snorted and lurched her powerful legs towards the door. Hundr held onto her mane with his right hand and narrowly avoided flying over her back as she sprang forward.

The mare burst through the barn door at a canter forcing Hundr to duck his head under the lintel. The horse cannoned out into the daylight, and Hundr found himself in a square which ran between the barns and the timber house. Across from him, four men stood, armed with spears and one with a hunting bow. Hundr flashed a grin at them and dug his heels again, wheeling the beast towards the open fields and back towards the forest line. He daren't go further inland, fearing what kind of Frankish settlements or warriors he might encounter. Hundr whooped as the mare picked up pace and the wind ran through his hair. An arrow flew past him but well wide, and he allowed himself a laugh. Things were looking up. He had a sack of food and a horse to put some distance between him and Ivar's hunters.

Racing towards the tree line and clutching his sack, Hundr craned his neck over his shoulder but the farmers were nowhere to be seen. He imagined they had run half-heartedly into the fields, but Hundr knew what he was, and even though there were four of them, they wouldn't chase a one-eyed warrior clad in mail and armed with two blades. His mail Brynjar alone would likely be enough to buy the whole farmstead. He turned back and almost slipped from the horse's back as the glint of sun on steel caught his eye from the treeline. A long line of warriors burst from the trees and ran towards him - Ivar's warriors.

Hundr yanked on the mare's mane and veered her to the left, running parallel to the farm and parallel to Ivar's forces. He risked a glance to his right and saw a green cape darting from behind a tall elm tree. Hundr swung his sack and grinned at his enemy, enjoying the anger he knew would spread across Ivar's handsome face. Hundr sped away, knowing they couldn't catch him. It would be a simple thing now to put distance between him and Ivar's men. *But where to go? I need to find safety for five more days until Einar returns.*

Hundr remembered the tale the captives had told on the deck of the warship, that ship of Northmen he had slaughtered only a day earlier.

They told of a Viking Lord, Haesten, the famous voyager, who was in Frankia at war and fighting alongside a Frankish Lord. The captives had said Haesten's forces were upriver, and so Hundr headed in that direction. He could add his sword to Haesten's forces for a few days, escape Ivar, and then loop back to meet Einar and the Seaworm crew.

It all seemed too easy as he allowed the mare to slow to a canter. His enemies were behind him, and a new war was in front. All he had to do was stay alive for five more days.

SIX

The Sun crept across the sky, reaching the mid-day point of her inevitable journey across the heavens. The sky was a bright powder blue, with only a light hazing of cloud, which allowed the gentle heat of the Sun to warm Hundr's face and dry his clothes. He allowed the big plough mare to plod along, and he swayed in time with her movements, riding comfortably on her back. He dipped into the sack taken from the barn and tore strips of dried ham hungrily until his belly was full.

Ivar's warriors could not keep pace with Hundr now that he was mounted, and he had seen or heard nothing of them since Ivar had burst through the forest's edge. Half the morning had passed since that encounter, and Hundr felt confident he had put enough distance between himself and them to not have to worry about their pursuit any longer. He knew Ivar would not travel too far from his ships. Without them, he would be stranded in Frankia, but there was still the risk that Ivar would sail the Windspear up-river and try to head him off.

With five days left to survive until he was to meet Einar, Hundr wondered if it was indeed a good idea to push on to find Haesten's forces, or if he should ride on for the rest of the day and then double back. If he doubled back, he would avoid Ivar's forces if they were indeed waiting for him upstream. Hundr decided it was a fool's game to second guess the Boneless, who had years of war experience behind him, so he would stick with the plan to find Haesten's army. Although he had given his commitment to Einar to help him raid and gather silver, the prospect of finding Haesten and his army made Hundr feel like he was continuing on his path. When he had run away from his home in the east, his dream was to become a warrior of reputation. Hundr knew from his time in England that war provided opportunity. There would be battles, sieges, and conflict. These were the situations where a warrior could show his mettle and build his name, so, although he risked capture and torture at Ivar's hands, Hundr rode towards Haesten with hope.

The first sign of Haesten's forces came in the late afternoon, as Hundr and his mare plodded across a pasture field dotted here and there with fat-bellied cows who glanced nonchalantly in his direction. That field sloped down into a shallow valley where small thatched dwellings bordered a thin river, and the land sloped away sharply into a range of hills. Across the river and on the slope, which had a brown hue interspersed with silvery-grey boulders, Hundr saw a column of five mounted men picking their way across the high ground. Each man had a long spear held upright, so their column looked like a spiked caterpillar crawling across the hillside. Hundr continued to ride parallel to that column. They were too far away for him to be sure they were Northmen, and they could just as easily be Franks patrolling their Lord's estates. If what the survivors of the slaughtered crew said was correct, then any Franks would not be searching for, nor in conflict with Haesten's forces, because Haesten fought alongside a Frankish Lord against a neighbouring kingdom. The prisoners hadn't known the ins and outs of that conflict, but Hundr wanted to make sure that if he came in contact with armed men, that they were at least Northmen. Once he found a Viking force, his next challenge would be to convince them he was a warrior for hire and that they should allow him to join their ranks. Northmen were naturally suspicious of masterless men; all men served a Lord somewhere. Any men who didn't were outcasts, likely criminals or losers in a feud gone bad somewhere, or some other reason indicating ill luck or ill humour.

Riding parallel to the column of spearmen, Hundr concocted a story for himself. A tale to convince the Northmen to let him join them, so he could join their ranks for five days and be safe. Then, he would simply slip away and follow the river back to the island and meet the Seaworm. He was deep in thought and chewing on his last piece of ham when a shout rang out behind him. His head snapped around as two mounted warriors emerged from the forest. The density of that woodland had steadily reduced as the day wore on, and it was now only a collection of glades and briars which separated farmland from the riverbank. Hundr must have passed by those two men and not noticed, but they had noticed him.

"You are a Dane?" one man said. He had a patchy beard and slurred his words in the way a man did when he had lost most of his teeth.

"Not a Dane, but from the North," he replied.

"You sound like a Rus," said the second man, who sat straight in the saddle and looked to be a tall man. "What are you doing here?"

Hundr knew if he gave the wrong answer to these men, they would drag him to their Lord as a prisoner or simply kill him on the spot for his mail and weapons.

"Thanks to Thor and Odin," Hundr said, offering the warriors a wide smile, "My name is Jarl

Rune Snorrisson. My ship was attacked upriver. Bastards were Northmen like us. I was on my way to join Jarl Haesten." Hundr said. He looked the warriors in the eye.

"Where're your men, then?" said Gaptooth.

"Lord," said Hundr.

"What?"

"Are you a Jarl?" said Hundr, in the haughtiest voice he could muster.

The two warriors looked at each other and then back at Hundr. He dropped his smile and frowned over his one eye. If this lie was going to work, then Hundr knew he had to take it all the way. Any Jarl would not take kindly to be questioned by Carls or simple warriors of another Jarl or Lord. Hundr saw Gaptooth glance at the sword at his hip, his mail, and the weapon on his back. Hundr looked like a Jarl, a filthy Jarl riding an unsaddled horse, but a well-armed and wealthy Jarl all the same.

"No, Lord," said Gaptooth, and Hundr nodded.

"My men are dead, killed by our attackers. I alone survived. My ship is downriver, stripped of anything valuable and littered with the corpses of my men. How far away is Lord Haesten?"

"Half a day's ride upriver, you can be there before nightfall," said the taller man.

"My thanks to you both. Shall we ride to his

camp together?"

"We are on patrol, Lord. Those men will lead you to Jarl Haesten," said Gaptooth, and he pointed his spear towards the valley basin. The column of spearmen from the hill had ridden down the valley and across the thin river whilst Hundr was talking to Gaptooth. They approached at a canter, bristling with weapons and Viking arrogance.

They rode up the slope towards Hundr in an arc, so they came on in a line. The leader reined in between Hundr and Gaptooth. He patted his horse's neck with his free hand and rested his spear against his horse's flank. The leader had hair so fair it was white, and his eyes were piercing blue so that his eyebrows looked like a shelf of snow above frozen pools of ice. His face was angular and long, giving him a look of cleverness and guile.

"Who is this?" said the leader.

Gaptooth sat straighter in the saddle.

"This is Jarl Rune Snorrison. His ship was attacked upriver."

The leader eyed Hundr carefully, and Hundr nodded in greeting.

"I stole this nag from a Frankish farm. My attackers were chasing me, the men who took my ship and killed my men. I was on my way to join

Jarl Haesten."

"I will bring you to him," said the leader. He arched an eyebrow at Hundr and clicked his tongue, urging his horse forwards. Hundr followed behind the column as they rode on.

Hundr followed the column in silence as they wound their way across fields and farms. He supposed, and hoped, that his story was believable. It was not beyond the realm of possibility that the Jarl of the ship Hundr had attacked might have survived the attack and scrambled to shore. After a short time, the leader of the company held up his hand, and the column fell in alongside him. The white-haired leader gestured through a wild section of brambles towards where the river flowed in the distance, visible from Hundr's position only as a sliver of sparkling blue in the distance.

Six men were at the river's edge, armed men. Hundr felt a knot tightening in his stomach and heat rising into his face. They could be Ivar's men, but it was too hard to tell from this distance.

"Are they ours?" asked the man next to Hundr, but the leader shook his head.

"No horses, either Franks or something else," said Whitehair, and as he spoke, he cast a lingering look at Hundr.

If they were Ivar's men and talked to Whitehair,

Hundr knew his ruse would be up, and his life would be over. They could be Franks, enemies of Haesten, or Ivar's men. Either way, Hundr could see that to wait could mean death, and so he charged. He drew Ivar's sword Munin from his back and dug his heels into the mare's flanks. She pushed off at a canter, and Hundr grinned at the company leader as he rode away.

"Where the ..." the leader said.

"Attack, kill!" Hundr shouted over his shoulder, hoping to rouse the column into action.

His mare was at a gallop now, and she raced through the thickets. In only a few heartbeats, Hundr could see the faces of six men staring at him, slack-jawed and frozen in indecision. As he drew close, Hundr saw all six wore their hair short and shaved close to their skulls. *Not Ivar's men, thank Odin.* They were Franks, and Hundr was sick of running.

He cannoned into the first Frank, his mare knocking the warrior from his feet, and Hundr wheeled the mare around, gripping her mane, and slashed down with Munin, feeling her tip bang into the skull of a second Frank. They filled the air with shouting, and the iron smell of blood was in the mare's nostrils. She whinnied and balked, so Hundr slid from her back and spun around her flank. A spear blade came for his face, and he ducked below it, rising from a crouch and ramming Munin into the belly of the spear-man. Three Franks were down, half of the enemy force, and Whitehair and his men had not yet joined the attack.

Hundr drew Soulstealer from her scabbard and turned to face the three remaining Franks with his two swords poised and ready to strike. The Franks spoke to him hurriedly, hands raised and babbling in a tongue he didn't understand. They looked frantically from Hundr to the ap-proaching column of Northmen. Hundr lunged at the closest man with Soulstealer, but the three Franks looked at one another, dropped their spears, and ran down the riverbank. White-hair rode past at the gallop, flanked by his men, and they pursued the three survivors. Hundr sheathed his blades and watched as the mounted men cut down the fleeing Franks with ease. He breathed a sigh of relief. Thank Odin, these were not Ivar's men.

Of the three men Hundr had cut down, two were still alive, but Hundr left them where they lay writhing on the ground. They were soldiers, and fighting was their living, so he felt no pity for their pain.

"You should not have attacked like that," said Whitehair as he returned to the scene of the fight. His blue eyes flashed under creased brows. "These men could have been our allies."

"Are they?" said Hundr.

"No, lucky for you."

"So we killed six of the enemy today, and we have good news to bring to Jarl Haesten."

Whitehair leaned forward in his saddle and spat across his horse's neck.

"I give the orders, Jarl," he said and looked Hundr up and down. "I'll bring you to Lord Haesten, but watch yourself. There could have been fifty men hidden here along the riverbank, or they could have been our Frankish allies. Just stay at the rear of my men. We will be with the Jarl before nightfall."

Hundr inclined his head to Whitehair. He had at least shown that he could fight, but it was clear Whitehair was sceptical about Hundr's story. It didn't matter, Hundr supposed. Once Whitehair brought him to Haesten, and he could sleep safely with his army for a few nights, that was all Hundr needed. He didn't need Whitehair's respect or friendship. Hundr went to retrieve his mare from where she cropped lazily at tall grass amongst the riverbank briar, and Whitehair's men dispatched the wounded Franks. They searched the dead and took anything of value. One of Whitehair's men tossed Hundr a skin of ale, and he drank deeply, thanking the man.

Whitehair was correct, and just as the sky darkened and shadows grew long, the column of riders turned inland, and the land before them was littered with campfires and the hum and noise of Haesten's army. It reminded Hundr of the Ragnarsson camp at York, where he had scaled the walls and fought side by side with Ivar the Boneless in the time before they were enemies. Whitehair rode through the camp, and Hundr could see that the river had in fact turned in this direction, and beyond the hustle and bustle of men and tents, he could see a cluster of tall masts in the distance, masts beyond count. Haesten had brought a fleet to Frankia and had made his camp at the river's edge.

"Wait here," Whitehair growled as he dismounted and strode off in the river's direction. Hundr slid off the mare and waited. As he waited, he watched the warriors come and go. Men laughed and drank ale. Some were marching off on patrol, and others still were making fires to keep warm in the night ahead.

"Jarl Rune?" said a stocky, balding warrior from across Hundr's shoulder. He turned and nodded at the man.

"Come, I will bring you to meet Jarl Haesten."

SEVEN

Jarl Haesten approached, walking with quick, short steps. He wore a coat of shining fish scale armour which shimmered gold as he marched. Haesten had a gold pommelled sword strapped to his waist and also a plainer, more workman-like axe hanging from a loop at the other side of his belt. He wore a thick gold chain about his neck. Everything about the man radiated wealth and power.

They instructed Hundr to wait beside the hull of a long Drakkar warship, which the Vikings had pulled half ashore. Haesten's men had erected a tent across the deck, just as they would on sea voyages at night and to keep out the rain and seawater. Hundr leant against the hull of that ship, but he pushed himself upright as the Jarl approached. Whitehair flanked Haesten, and another, older warrior with greying hair tied back from a nut-brown scarred face. Haesten himself was not a tall man, Hundr guessed he stood a hand taller than him. Haesten shared the pure white hair of the man at his side, but Haestens was cut close-cropped to his head and stood up like a brush from his forehead. He had pale blue eyes and an angular, clean-shaven face.

"So, you are Jarl Rune?" Haesten said in a clear, confident voice. He came to a stop and tucked his hands into his sword belt, which was studded with gold and iron rivets. *All Einar needs to do is kill Haesten, and he could buy all the land he could ever need.*

"Greetings, Jarl Haesten," Hundr said, inclining his head respectfully. "I have heard of your campaign and your reputation, and so I brought my ship to join your forces."

"My brother Erik here," Haesten waved a hand toward Whitehair next to him, "is dubious of your claims. He fears you are a masterless man. Come here perhaps as a spy sent by my enemies."

Erik shifted from foot to foot and spat at Hundr's feet. Hundr held Haesten's gaze, and the steely ferocity behind those pools of blue reminded him of Ivar. Clearly, the Jarl was a man of few words, the briskness of his approach and the brusque tone showed, clearly, that Haesten was a busy man. Which he must be, Hundr assumed, with a war to organise and men to command.

"You say I am a liar?" Hundr said, doing his best to look affronted at such an insult.

"Aye, you're no Jarl," said Erik.

"So we'll fight then, you and I, and Odin will decide the truth of it," Hundr said. It was a risk challenging Haesten's brother, but Hundr had to prove his claim, or Haesten would likely kill him where he stood. Also, Hundr welcomed combat. Amongst Northmen, any warrior could challenge another to fight a Holmgang to settle a dispute. He wanted to fight. Ever since leaving Northumbria, his only solace lay in combat. He could focus his mind on the fight at hand and push away the thoughts of Saoirse, Sten, and the pain of his torture. Haesten's brother took a step forward, and Hundr placed his hand on Soulstealer's hilt. Haesten and the other warrior stepped back and touched the hilts of their own blades. The grey-haired man raised his hand, motioning for calmness.

"I come to you in friendship to lend my blades to yours. My ship was attacked, and my crew slaughtered. This man brings me here, knowing I am a Jarl, and doesn't even offer his own name. Now I am called a liar. Is this your hospitality?" said Hundr. He was in deep now and had to keep the momentum of his effrontery moving.

Haesten placed a hand on his brother's arm.

"Jarl Rune, perhaps my brother was hasty in his allegations," said Haesten.

Hundr nodded and took his hand from his

sword.

"But you are right, and you will fight to prove the truth of your words," Haesten said, and his eyes bore deeper into Hundr's, searching for fear or doubt, but there was none. Haesten's white eyebrows turned up at the centre, digging deep frown lines into his forehead and his jaw jutted, open-mouthed and pensive.

"Very well, I am ready," Hundr said, and he drew Soulstealer from his waist scabbard and Munin from his back. He grinned at Erik, but Haesten's brother did not take the bait.

"You won't fight Erik. You will fight my champion. That will test the truth of your words," Haesten said, and now Erik smiled at Hundr, a mirthless and flat smile. Hundr nodded. He didn't care who he would fight. The obvious irony was that Erik was right, Hundr was lying about his name and status. He only hoped the fight would come soon and allow him to escape his own mind for a time.

"I put my trust in Odin then. I'll fight whomever you choose, Jarl Haesten. Your brother here, or your champion."

Haesten frowned and nodded. "We'll gather the men first. They'll want to see the Holmgang. If you win, then you are who you say you are, and we will be friends, you and I. If you lose, well..." he said with a shrug.

Either outcome suited Haesten. The spectacle of the Holmgang would please his men and keep morale high amid whatever war was afoot here in Frankia. If Hundr lost, it was nothing to Haesten. Hundr was just one man with no crew to strengthen the Jarl's numbers. If Hundr won, which he assumed Haesten thought unlikely, then Haesten lost one champion but gained another.

Hundr had fought a Holmgang before. He had fought Toki in a roughly made square of branches in Northumbria to earn his place as a warrior on Einar's crew. Before that, his place on the crew had been as a bailing boy, responsible for bailing the bilge with a bucket when at sea. Hundr had won that fight; he had won easily, having deceived Toki into believing he had no skill at arms. That ruse bought Hundr a few moments and the element of surprise, which he had used to defeat Toki and earn his place amongst Einar's warriors. That ploy would not work this time. Hundr was trying to pass himself off as a Jarl, who, as a wealthy nobleman, would have been taught to use spear and axe from the time he could walk.

Evening drew in, and the shroud of darkness covered the world as Haesten's warriors gathered in a wide field behind their camp. Tradition and rules usually surrounded the fighting of a Holmgang. It was a legal right, and the result of the fight carried the weight of law for Northmen. They made a square of hazel rods placed on the ground, and each warrior should have a second and an agreed-upon number of replacement shields. In the north, where a Holmgang could settle disputes over land and inheritance, as well as insults, the fight would be more ritualised. In his home in the east, Hundr had seen duels arranged even three or four days after a challenge was made. There would be a feast and celebrations and an animal sacrifice on the day of combat. Haesten, however, was a man in a rush, and so Hundr would fight his champion that very evening on a torch-lit field.

"One shield, no seconds. Fight to the death," Erik said simply as he handed Hundr a shield and took his place beside his brother on the square's edge. One shield and a fight to the death suited Hundr. If he won, he would surely have a safe bed for the night and four more days to stay alive before the Seaworm returned. If he died, then he would be free of Saoirse and Sten's torment and would take his place in Valhalla.

Cheering erupted amongst the gathered warriors, and the press of men across from Hundr parted to make space for Haesten's champion. Hundr's breath caught in his throat as he saw the colossal figure striding towards him. The man stood head and shoulders above any of the gathered warriors, taller even than Sten Slegyya,

Hundr thought. What so shocked Hundr, however, was that this warrior's skin was as black as
the night sky. He was stripped to the waist, and
muscles rippled beneath the man's dark skin as
he stalked through the crowd. Hundr had never
seen a man so dark before. He had heard of such
men, blámen or blue men from the far south,
where few men dared to sail.

The warrior reached the centre of the Holmgang square and fixed Hundr with a baleful stare.
He had a long-handled war axe in one hand, and
a shield in the other. The huge warrior took his
place opposite Hundr, and without delay, Haesten clapped his hands, signalling that the duel
could begin.

Hundr gripped the wooden handle in the bowl
of his shield and drew Munin from her scabbard at his back. He was confident in his fighting
skill, but the appearance and size of his opponent
knotted his guts. He swallowed hard and ignored
the sudden urge to piss. Hundr brought Munin
to his lips and kissed the smoke-patterned blade.
*I took this blade from Ivar the Boneless, Champion
of the North. Bring me luck.* Hundr puffed out his
cheeks and went to meet his fate.

The huge dark-skinned warrior bellowed, raising his head and shouting to the heavens. Then
he launched himself at Hundr, swinging the axe
as effortlessly as though it were a twig. Hundr
raised his shield, and the axe blade thudded

into the boards, driving Hundr's arm backwards. Such was the force of the blow that the axe stuck into the shield's timber, and the warrior yanked to pull it free. His strength was incredible, and he dragged Hundr from his feet and swung him around like a child's rag doll. Hundr let go of the shield before his enemy ripped his arm from its socket, and he tumbled to the grass, rolling and stumbling to his knees. The warriors around the square howled with laughter, and Hundr watched his opponent put one foot on the shield and drag his blade free. He dropped his axe, picked up the broken shield, and launched it at Hundr. The shield flew low and flat, and Hundr dived out of the way to avoid it. He rolled to his feet again and glanced behind him to where the shield had clattered into the crowd, bringing three men down. The crowd was in a frenzy now, whooping and cheering at the ferocity of their champion.

Hundr swallowed hard. He drew Soulstealer from her fleece-lined scabbard and took a deep breath. A blade in each hand suited Hundr. He felt balanced and never enjoyed fighting with a shield. He liked to attack, not cower behind the linden boards. Hundr strode towards his foe, and the man swung his axe in a wide arc to meet Hundr's approach. This time, however, Hundr swayed back from that arc and allowed the blade to hiss by harmlessly. The momentum of that swing twisted the man's torso wide, and Hundr darted forwards and sliced Soulstealer across the exposed rib cage and then ducked under the returning axe swing. Hundr's heart leapt as the huge warrior yelped in pain. The axe was too big, and it made the man slow. Hundr was sure that the sheer terror of the huge warrior combined with the frightening size of the axe blade was usually enough to subdue most men, but Hundr had fought against big men before and won. He was not afraid of death; he even welcomed the peace it would bring.

Hundr drove the attack, stabbing and slashing with his swords in a blur of fury and skill. His opponent parried some strikes, dodged others, but his skin was cut in half a dozen places, and his blood flowed and dripped on the grass, its deep red looking black in the flickering torchlight of the Holmgang square. The huge warrior was panting, his eyes wide and staring at Hundr's scar ravaged face. Hundr leapt forwards again and feinted with his right hand, then with his left slashed at his enemy's thigh. The warrior fell to one knee with a gasp, and Hundr brought his knee crashing into the man's face, dropping him to the turf. The warrior groaned and tried to rise, but Hundr punched him twice in the face with the pommel of his sword, putting his foe to sleep.

Moments earlier, shouts and roars filled the night sky. But now the gathered crowd stood silent, so quiet that Hundr heard an owl hooting in a far off tree. He turned to point his two blades at Erik and Haesten.

"I speak the truth. My victory proves that truth," he growled, and Erik's face twisted into a grimace, his white eyebrows standing out in the darkness.

"Very well, Jarl Rune, you speak the truth, and I welcome you to our army."

Hundr nodded thanks and pointed his sword at the fallen warrior.

"He fights well, your blámen, and I spare his life. It's a waste of life to kill such a fine warrior for sport. I'd be honoured to stand with him in a shield wall."

"I'm sure he will thank you for that. Now, let's eat together. Tomorrow we march to meet our enemies, and you will join us. All the crew should drink and feast tonight. It will be the last chance for a while," Haesten said, and the gathered warriors cheered again.

Hundr sighed and sheathed his swords. He had survived another day and would surely now be safe for the night. *So, four more days to stay alive.*

EIGHT

Einar leant against the Seaworm's stern. He breathed deeply and slowly, with one hand resting on the tiller and one hand over his stomach. He spent most of his time standing in this way; it was the only position other than lying flat on his back, where he was not in pain. There was a fresh wind blowing south which filled the Seaworm's sail, and Einar turned his head to allow the wind to blow through his long, braided hair and enjoyed its freshness across his face.

A stab of pain lanced his guts, so Einar pulled himself upright and winced, cursing softly to himself. The wound was deep and terrible, and Einar was more than aware that had it not been for the healing skills of Ragnhild, Hildr, and Hrist, then he would have died. Their skill at healing matched the Valkyrie warrior priestess' skill in battle and ferocity, and Einar owed them his life.

Einar's shoulders shuddered involuntarily as the memory of terrible suffering flooded his thoughts. He remembered it in fleeting episodes, his time lying under the rowing benches of the Seaworm, sweating and writhing in agony. Time had been a fluid thing, slipping in and out of consciousness, travelling far into the dream world. His mind was plagued with visions of the men he had killed, their faces splattered with blood and screaming into his face as they took revenge upon him through his dreams. Those men wailed of wives left destitute, sons and daughters sold into slavery, and fathers and mothers bereft at the loss of a son they loved and would never see again. Such was the life of a warrior, Einar had been told when he was a child. You risk death when you take to the whale-road, so you either accept that risk, or stay in the Northlands and till the fields or shepherded the livestock. Einar had happily accepted that risk for many years. More than that, he loved battle. He revelled in his reputation as Einar the Brawler. Einar was Ivar's dog of war, and the Boneless would send him on the most difficult of tasks. He would sail to Ivar's many holdings, in Ireland, in the Orkney Islands, or up North in the homelands. Einar would punish men sworn to Ivar but who did not pay their dues or send men when commanded.

Many men had suffered under Einar's axe, and until now, he had never cared for their fate. They all knew and took the same risks as he when embarking on a life at sea in pursuit of silver and reputation. But all that changed the day Ivar plunged a hand's length of cold sword iron deep into Einar's guts. The blade was cold and sharp, biting into Einar's body like some pitiless monster's claw. Ivar had twisted the blade and pulled it free, and that was when the pain began. White-hot, unspeakable pain. Einar remembered holding his own entrails into his body to stop them from spilling out on that Northumbrian jetty where he had fought Ivar and lost. His guts were slick and smooth in his hands, the pain searing and blinding. Hundr had pulled Einar back from the fight and then fought and defeated Ivar himself.

Many times, as he lay prostrated and racked with the pain from his wound, Einar wished they had left him to die that day. He had fallen to Ivar the Boneless, the Champion of the North, and had done so with his hand gripping his axe. Einar was sure that his place in Valhalla was already earned He would have died fighting with honour against a great warrior, and he had fought in the front line his whole life, sending many souls to Odin for his Einherjar. Einar looked at the white-tipped waves of the vast sea before him. On a cloudy day like this, it was a surging brown mass of power and force, not the green, blue pool of a sun-drenched afternoon. Dying that day would have been a fitting end to his life. He would have gone with pride and waited in Odin's hall for Ivar and his other friends and enemies to feast and fight until the day of Ragnarök. Instead, the Valkyrie had stitched his guts together. The gods only knew how they had done it. The wound had become infected and reeked of the rot, but they had brought him through it. Months later, Einar had become strong enough to stand, though thin and frail, a shadow of his former self. So now he was alive, denied his place in Valhalla. He would live and perhaps grow old. Through the long nights and days lying alone, he had cried like a child amidst the pain and mind-bending visions. All he had craved then was a hand to hold, someone to pull him close and tell him it would all be alright. These were shameful thoughts for a drengr, a warrior, but Einar was beyond all that now. If he was going to grow old, then he needed someone to share his life with, a wife and maybe some children. Or he would find the glorious death that would take him to Valhalla. To get that, however, he needed to fight. His stomach twisted at the thought of facing a blade again.

"We'll have to go ashore for food, Lord," came the familiar voice of Bush, rousing Einar from his thoughts. Einar looked at his old friend. He was a short but sturdy man, with a heavy paunch hanging over his belt and bald save for a ring of long hair which ran around below the bottom of his skull but went no higher than his ears at any point. Bush kept his baldness covered with a stained leather helmet liner, which he rarely took off. Bush's prize possession was a magnificent helmet, well-crafted and ringed with runic inscriptions, but he kept that precious piece of gear well hidden under his rowing bench.

"We passed a place this morning which looked quiet. We'll come about tomorrow and head back that way," said Einar. Bush nodded and took the liner from his head to scratch at his scalp, which was as white as a fresh hen's egg from so rarely seeing the sun.

"So we just keep sailing around this river for a week?"

"We do. After today we've got four more days before we go back for him."

"What if Ivar comes back upriver?"

"We don't have enough men to fight, not against Ivar's two crews," said Einar with a shrug, "so we keep our eyes peeled and the wind in our sail."

"Supposing the lad has outfoxed Ivar and he's there when go back. What then?"

"Then we go Viking again."

"For more silver?"

Einar nodded. "For more silver. Enough for us to get what we want, Bush."

"To settle down, find some peace," Bush said. He searched Einar's eyes and then tore his own away to look at his boots.

"Find wives, have some children. Drink some ale and get fat."

"We've sailed and fought together for a long time. Always we've lived by our blades and been rewarded with silver and arm rings."

"We have."

"Well, me and the lads have been talking, and ..."

"You and the lads?"

"Yes, me, Blink, Brownlegs."

"Talking about what?"

"About settling down and all that."

"And?"

"As much as we'd love to have pretty wives and halls and warm fires, we just aren't farmers. We're warriors."

Einar frowned at his old friend. "You think we can fight forever? Crooked-backed and toothless old men fighting in the shield wall? It can't go on forever, Bush, we'll be butchered."

"But we've always known that, Lord. We always thought we would go out in battle, blade in hand and on to Valhalla or Thor's mighty hall, Thruth-vangar."

"What if you don't die in battle? What if you die without a Lord and alone begging for scraps somewhere?" Einar said. Bush nodded and smiled, that lipless smile when a man knows there isn't any point in continuing a conversation.

Einar looked at the sea, and a silent moment passed between them, the comfortable silence only possible between friends. His wound jabbed and lanced pain across his midriff, and Einar grimaced. It didn't matter what Bush said. They would raid and find enough silver, and Einar would buy some land. Grow old in peace. To get to Valhalla now would mean standing in the shield wall again, facing the sharp slashing blade of an enemy who wants to hurt you, to make you bleed and weep for your life. The strike from an axe or sword doesn't always kill. Einar had seen more than one old warrior, having lost an arm, leg, or blinded in some distant battle and reduced to begging for scraps outside his Lord's hall until the nithing death took him to walk the afterlife as a wraith without honour. There was no guarantee of Valhalla. So a warm fire and a wife to hold in the darkness was what lay in Einar's future, of that he was sure.

"What do you make of the new lads?" said Bush, nodding his head towards Guthmund and the others, huddled together at the other end of the ship.

"They know their business," said Einar, which was true. Guthmund and the new crew members were fine sailors and knew the ins and outs of a longship.

"I don't trust them."

"Why not?"

"They're too shifty. Always whispering and sneaking about the deck. And there's nearly as many of them as there are of us."

Bush was right. Guthmund and the new men weren't exactly men who instilled confidence in their trustworthiness. They stuck together and had mixed little with the old crew, and Einar wasn't blind to the risk of a knife in the dark in the backs of the old crew. It wouldn't be too difficult for Guthmund to take the Seaworm if he put his mind to it.

"Keep an eye on them. Talk to Ragnhild and the others. We need them, Bush. We can't sail the ship with just the old crew. There's not enough of us to man the oars."

Einar leant on the tiller to keep the Seaworm from heading too close landward. As the ship came about, Einar saw sails in the distance.

"Sails," he shouted, and Bush jumped across the deck, swinging around the rigging to peer over the side.

"Odin's balls. Ten ships, Lord, warships."

Bush was right. They weren't the fat-bellied tubs built by the Franks or Saxons. These ships cut through the sea like knives. Sleek and smooth, snarling beasts at their prows, growling at the world in defiance.

"Can you see their sails?" Einar said.

Bush raised his hand to his forehead to shield his eyes and peered at the flotilla.

"I'm too bloody old. My eyes have gone to shit," said Bush. "Hjalmar," he called to one of the new crew members. "What's on their sails?"

Hjalmar peered across the waves, his younger eyes seeing clearly and further than Bush or Einar could manage.

"Raven. They carry the Raven banner on their sails."

"Raven, are you sure?" said Einar.

"Yes, Lord. A white Raven on a black sail, all of them."

"It can't be Ivar's ships, they're all fighting the Saxons. Same for Ubba Ragnarsson and the Snake Eye," said Bush.

The sons of Ragnar Lothbrok all flew the famous raven banner. It wasn't any of the sons who fought in Saxon England, there was only one other son permitted to fly the Raven.

"It's Ironside. Bjorn Ironside is here."

****

Hundr sat across from Haesten in the Jarl's tent, which stretched across his warship, Wave Falcon. Erik sat next to his brother, along with two other high-ranking Jarls in Haesten's army. There was a small brazier where logs crackled, and plates filled with roast mutton and beef sat perched on stools, along with pots of ale and hunks of cheese. Hundr ate his fill and drank deeply of the sweetly delicious ale.

"You fight well," said Jarl Arne between mouthfuls of cheese, the crumbs of which littered his bushy red beard.

"We all thought that demon of yours was impossible to defeat," said Jarl Knut. He was a thin man with a weasel-sharp face. They introduced him to Hundr as the Jarl of the small isles off the coast of western Norway.

"I'm surprised we haven't heard of you, Jarl Rune, with such fighting prowess," said Haesten. He drank from a horn cup of ale but never took his blue eyes off Hundr's. Hundr nodded his thanks to the three Jarls and stuffed his mouth with gloriously fatty mutton, hoping a full mouth would lessen the need for him to talk.

"Where did you say your lands are?" asked Knut.

I didn't.

"East," he said between mouthfuls, "East of Jutland." He held up a finger to excuse himself from being unable to talk with so much food in his mouth. He swallowed and washed the meat down with a draught of ale. The three Jarls stared at him, leaning forward on their stools, waiting for him to elaborate. "Tell me more about this war with the Franks," said Hundr, trying to change the course of the conversation as deftly as possible.

The two Jarls looked sideways at Haesten, and the silence dragged on for an awkward moment as Haesten would not deign to give the tale himself.

"We are here to fight alongside Salomon, Duke of Brittany. He fights against another Frankish Duke, Robert the Strong," said Knut.

"A duke is a Jarl, but with more power, lots of land and men," said Arne, having seen Hundr's raised eyebrow in response to the unfamiliar words.

"What are they fighting about?" asked Hundr.

"What men always fight about. Land and power," said Haesten. He murmured, almost in a whisper.

"How do you know this Duke Salomon?"

"Haesten came across him upon his return from the South, and needing to replenish his resources, he..."

Haesten turned to glare at Knut as he spoke, and Knut stopped talking as those pale eyes bore into him. Haesten's brows knitted together, furrowing his forehead.

"We voyaged south, far south, farther than men have ever sailed before. To where men's skins are dark like Kolo whom you fought today," said Erik. "There was a storm, a monstrous thing of Njorth's fury, and it tore half of our fleet asunder." He stopped and looked at his brother, and Haesten stared at the brazier, his thoughts on some distant sea, remembering whatever horror they had endured.

"Twenty ships gone, hard men taken by Njorth to the depths of the sea," Haesten whispered.

"Along with most of the silver and gold taken from the voyage," said Knut.

Haesten's head snapped around, "I've won more silver and more glory than the rest of the North combined. I've sailed further and fought harder than any man alive." Haesten was shaking, his knuckles white where he squeezed his cup, and his eyes bulging. Erik put a hand on his brother's shoulder, and Haesten took a drink. He mastered himself and stared into the flames, open-mouthed and jaw jutting.

"You have seen the heat of the battle too," said Erik, pointing to Hundr's missing eye. Hundr touched at his face absently. Sometimes, when the pain subsided, he forgot how ravaged his face was. A long angry red scar ran down his face from forehead to chin, and his left eye was a dark, angry pit. His eyelid was half-closed permanently, and beneath it there was only despair. Brownlegs had tried to convince him to wear an eye patch more than once, claiming that the sight of Hundr's face put the men off their food.

"So I have. I fought for a while in Northumbria, alongside the sons of Ragnar," he said. "Which is where I heard of you, Jarl Haesten. So I came here to join your forces and share the glory."

The other men nodded. Knut leant towards Hundr as though he wanted to learn more about the war against the Saxons, but Arne touched his arm gently and, as Knut turned to him, Arne shook his head. Haesten was still red-faced, staring into the flames and breathing deeply. There was silence in the tent now, and Hundr could hear the laughter and singing of the men in the camp outside, enjoying the last feast before the march to war began. Hundr banged his fist against his chest and belched. He stood and walked towards the tent entrance. The Jarls didn't ask why he left, and he didn't excuse himself. He knew he had to get out of there before they probed him more about his lands and home. Hundr hadn't thought through his story in enough detail to bear their scrutiny.

Outside of the tent, the air was fresh, and Hundr breathed it in deeply. He leant against the side and looked out across Haestens camp, where dozens of small fires blazed and men no doubt told stories of the Gods, their own deeds, and the glory they would earn on the campaign ahead. Hundr was suddenly aware of a presence ahead of him, and he took a pace forward, squinting into the darkness. There, only five paces away, the hulking warrior he had fought that day also leant on the ship's bows. He had dressings on his wounds, and he nodded his head in recognition of Hundr's presence.

"Is it sore?" Hundr said, pointing to the deepest wound, the one he had cut across the big man's side. The warrior, Kolo, as Erik had called him, drank from a horn of ale. He shook his hand, smiling, and nodded at the drink. Hundr smiled. "That will dull the pain."

Kolo returned his smile.

"Do you speak our tongue?"

"I do. I had to learn it. It is very different from the language of my people," Kolo said, his accent thick and strange.

"You are sworn to Haesten?"

"He bought me from my master, me and three others."

"So you are a slave?"

"Yes, I fight for Haesten because I have no choice."

"He is lucky to have you. It was an honour to fight you today," Hundr said, and offered his hand to the giant. Kolo looked at the hand and then laughed. They clasped forearms, and Kolo passed his ale horn to Hundr.

They drank in silence until a roar erupted from the camp downriver from the Wave Falcon.

"What is it?" said Hundr. He and Kolo looked across the camp where men rushed, cheering, towards the river's edge.

"Ships," said Kolo, "Lord Bjorn is here with his fleet, or what's left of it."

"Who is Bjorn?"

"Bjorn Ironside, Bjorn Ragnarsson."

Another son of Ragnar. Shit.

NINE

Bjorn Ironside arrived with ten warships filled with grizzled, battle-hardened Viking warriors. Bjorn himself was a bear of a man. Where his brother Ivar was handsome, lithe, and supple, Bjorn was huge, strong, and big-bearded. What Hundr found most surprising about Bjorn, however, was that where Ivar was baleful and malevolent, Bjorn was filled with joy and laughter, and the men loved him.

Hundr stood on the deck of the Wave Falcon along with Kolo, and they watched as Bjorn's ship rowed towards the river's shore. Haesten's warriors crowded on the riverbank and chanted "Ironside" over and over until the man himself leapt from his ship, landing in the water and slipping in the mud. He stood and roared with laughter, throwing his head back and his arms wide. He strode ashore and moved through the cheering masses. Bjorn clasped forearms with men, clapped them on the shoulder, and he dragged one little warrior into a bear hug, lifting the man from the ground, much to the enjoyment of the crowd.

Kolo smiled broadly and shook his head as they watched Bjorn's raucous reception.

"The men love him," said Hundr.

"All men love Bjorn, my friend. He is a madman. Generous too."

"He and Haesten are allies?"

"They are. They won a fortune together in the South. Then lost it on the way home."

"How?"

"When Haesten bought me, he and Bjorn had forty ships and had plundered the coast all around Ispanialand. On the way North, we hit ferocious storms, and twenty of those ships were lost."

"Is that your country, Ispanialand?"

Kolo laughed. "No, my home is far even to the South of that, my friend. A long way away."

"So, Haesten and Bjorn lost their wealth?"

"Which is why we are here, to find more."

Haesten, Erik, and two Jarls emerged from the tent, and Bjorn climbed a rope ladder to leap onto the Wind Falcon. His smile faded when he caught Haesten's eye, and the two men nodded solemnly at one another. Hundr saw something pass between them, a look of shared pain, shared respect, and brotherhood.

"Lord Haesten," said Bjorn in a deep voice. He stroked his long black bushy beard with a huge ham-sized hand.

"Lord Bjorn," said Haesten, and then they clasped forearms.

"What news?"

"You arrive just in time. The Franks have brought an army to meet us, only a day's march away," said Haesten.

"So we make the shield wall," said Bjorn, "Salomon is here?"

"No, he and his men march behind the Franks into their lands. Our task is to defeat this Robert the Strong and then march in behind Salomon and on into Frankia."

"Where there are fat cities and Christ Churches for the taking?"

"Just so," said Haesten, and he and Bjorn ducked into his tent.

"I thought we were in Frankia?" said Hundr.

"It's confusing, my friend," said Kolo, "We fight with Duke Salomon of Brittany, which is where we are now. It's sort of part of Frankia. Salomon fights with other Duke's deciding who rules

Frankia and who rules Brittany. I think."

"If we don't know why we are fighting, then why are we fighting?"

Kolo laughed again, "Haesten and Bjorn don't care who or why we are fighting. As long as there is silver and glory."

Which, Hundr supposed, was enough. Kolo was kind to Hundr, even though they had fought only that day, and Kolo still limped and groaned from his wounds. He allowed Hundr to share his quarters in a tent next to the Wind Falcon, where Haesten's picked men, his bodyguards, slept. Hundr could have asked for better quarters, something more befitting of a Jarl, but he liked Kolo. He was safe within the army now, and after this night, he had only three more days before he could head back upriver to Einar. Hundr supposed he could keep his head down, march with Kolo towards the fight in Frankia and then slip away to join his friends. There had been no sign of Ivar, or any talk of him in camp, which Hundr hoped would continue even though Ivar's brother, Bjorn, was Haesten's ally.

The army broke camp early that morning and had only marched for part of the day before Haesten's scouts sighted the enemy force. The Franks had drawn themselves up to offer battle on the slope of a hill leading away from the field where Hundr now stood in line. He had a borrowed shield strapped to his arm and his two swords at his waist and back. Hundr stood in the front rank next to Kolo and amongst Haesten's picked men.

"Looks like we're going to attack then," Hundr said, sniffing as he thought about climbing the hill ahead into the ranks of Frankish warriors.

"We go soon, my friend," said Kolo, "Bjorn likes to make speeches; he will talk, then we fight."

When he had jumped ship, Hundr had not envisaged fighting in a shield wall. All he had thought about was drawing Ivar away from the Seaworm. Yet here he was, ready to fight a battle which didn't concern him, and in which he was unlikely to receive any of the plunder if Haesten and Bjorn won. He hoped to be gone and safely at sea before the sacking of any towns or cities. If they won this battle.

"Have you fought in the shield wall before?"

"Many times, my friend. We are warriors. This is what we do," said Kolo.

"How are your wounds?"

"Scratches, nothing more. Do not worry yourself. We fight on the same side now," Kolo said and flashed a wide grin.

Whilst Hundr knew he must leave Kolo and Haesten soon, he had to admit that he enjoyed being part of the army. Since he had fought Kolo, and then befriended the giant, Hundr felt lighter, his memories pushed to the back of his mind by the new situation he found himself in. He stood now in the line of battle. He did not feel fear, but nor did he feel the hunger to launch himself into enemy blades to replace his troubles with battle joy. Kolo was a pleasant companion; he was a slave, and yet he did not carry that status heavily. Kolo was quick to laughter, and to share food and ale with Hundr. The new-found friendship was a welcome distraction, and made Hundr feel a part of something.

"Remind me why we are fighting again?" said Hundr, and Kolo laughed loudly, baring a set of glorious white teeth.

"Because this is where the battle is, my friend. One Frankish Duke wants to take land from another Frankish Duke. If we win, we get to take plump towns and churches."

"So we fight for wealth." Which was enough, Hundr supposed. It made him think about Einar. After Northumbria, he and Einar had sworn never to serve another Lord again, never to swear that oath of fealty. The only way to avoid the treachery and dishonour of others was to be the master of one's own destiny. But Hundr was here, on a damp midday in Frankia, about to fight for a Lord to which he had sworn no oath, for a Duke he had never heard of, and if he won, there would likely be more silver to be had than he and

Einar could take in two years of raiding aboard the Seaworm. To have that discussion with Einar meant Hundr had to survive, which meant getting through this battle and three more days.

A swirling wind surged down the hillside and carried with it the howls and battle songs of the Frankish ranks. A man on a fine, grey stallion rode up and down their battle lines waving a sword, and the warriors responded with war cries and clashed their weapons on the iron rims of their shields, first in spontaneous banging, but then the sound changed into a rhythmic drum sound, interspersed with a war song that undulated across the battlefield. Hundr heard a roar developing from the rear of the Vikings' own ranks, and he turned to see the lines of men parting like a wave crashing ashore. At the crest of that wave was Bjorn Ironside. He wore a full-faced helmet from which a long plume of white horsehair flowed behind him. As he marched, he cajoled the men. He nodded and called to warriors he recognised in the ranks. Bjorn hugged and bumped his mailed chest against others. The men loved him, and Hundr felt it too. He felt heat rising from his belly, and his heart quickened. He smiled, and he looked up to see Kolo was grinning at him. Beside Bjorn, Haesten marched in baleful silence. Where Bjorn was all weapon-shaking excitement, Haesten was anger and fury. Haesten marched with his head bowed, his chest heaving with deep breaths. He had a shield in one hand, painted with the falcon that was his banner, and an axe in the other. His gold pommelled sword was nowhere to be seen. He carried instead a plain workmanlike axe just the same as any regular carl of the army.

Haesten pushed himself into the front rank alongside Kolo, on the opposite side of Hundr. Bjorn stepped out in front of the army and waved his sword above his head and thrust the blade towards the enemy. The Viking lines gave a clipped roar and surged forward. Hundr felt a shield pushing at his back as the men behind grew excited and wanted to charge up the hill with wild abandon, but in such a charge lay slaughter and defeat.

"Hold. Hold the line," shouted Haesten, and the front rank, Hundr included, stiffened their backs and held the march at a regular pace to keep the ranks in order.

They took twenty steps and were upon the hill, ten more, and Hundr felt his thighs burn a little from the steep climb. The Franks had a clear advantage here. Hundr recalled the lessons from his masters in the East. Selecting the right terrain and battle conditions was a fundamental element of any warrior's education, and to attack uphill was not on the list of favourable conditions. The high ground gave the enemy the advantage of striking down on their attackers, and the oncoming force would spend much energy on the trudge uphill.

"Shield wall," Haesten shouted, and the warriors grunted as shields came up. Each man overlapped his shield with the man on his left, and the ranks behind lifted their shields overhead to rest on the rim of the shield in front.

"Arrows," came a warning from down the line. The Viking shield wall was just that, a wall of linden wood which held solid and allowed for an ordered advance and a protected attack. It was the standard attack and defence formation of any Viking force, and Northmen practiced the manoeuvres of the shield wall every day from the time they could lift the shield's weight.

Hundr heard the thuds of arrow strikes banging on shields around him. He kept his shield locked with Kolo's. His shoulder ached from the weight of the shield of the man behind him resting on his own shield's rim. A missile smashed into the lower half of Hundr's shield, and he grunted as the force of that blow banged the shield against his midriff, but he kept it raised, and they marched on. Hundr peered through the space between the shields. Bjorn Ironside was still capering beyond the shield wall, marching into the enemy missiles without shield or protection.

"Lothbrok, Lothbrok!" Bjorn shouted as he danced and brandished his sword. Lothbrok was his father, Ragnar's name. It meant hairy breeks in honour of the goatskin trews Ragnar wore to battle. It was a fearsome name. Ragnar was legendary among Northmen as a sacker of cities and hero without equal.

Hundr could see the bearded faces of the enemy now. Their shields were not as large as Viking shields, leaving their faces and shins exposed. The arrow strikes stopped as the Vikings grew closer, only to be replaced by a volley of spears. One spear struck Hundr's shield, driving him backwards a step, but luckily it fell away. A heavy spear stuck in a man's shield would drag it down, which was the point, to disrupt the shield wall of the Viking advance.

"Attack, kill them, kill them all," came the shout from Haesten. The Viking army bellowed as one, shaking the hillside with their fury. Hundr kept pace with Kolo as they quickened to a jog and then to a sprint. Hundr's heart thumped in his chest now, thighs and shoulders burning from the shield wall march up the hill. He risked another peek beyond his shield. Bjorn had launched himself into the Franks, cutting and slashing and screaming with wild ferocity.

Hundr clenched his teeth and braced his shoulder, and thundered into the Frankish line with a bone-jarring crunch. He shoved at the man in front, and that Frankish warrior shoved back. Hundr could feel the heat of his breath over the rim of his shield, and because that enemy was above him on the hill's slope, Hundr felt himself pushed backwards. A blade banged on the shield above his head, and a shining spear tip sneaked through the gap between his and Kolo's shield but did no damage.

"Now, kill them now!" Haesten roared. Daylight showed above Hundr where the man behind him removed his shield, and he felt the push in his back from that man as the army surged forwards. Hundr felt the calm descend, that familiar cloak of battle joy. He allowed himself a grin and raised his shield quickly, banging the rim into the attacking Frank's face. That bought Hundr a moment of space, and he crouched to slash at Frank's unprotected shins. As his enemy wailed in pain, Hundr roared and surged forward. He sliced Soulstealer upwards and dropped his shield, using the free hand to grab the shaft of the spear which had thrust wide of his shield, and he pulled that Frank forwards and off-balance into the Viking lines.

Hundr was amongst the enemy now. A blade sliced across his shoulder, but his mail deflected the blow. Hundr buried Soulstealer in the guts of a tall Frank, and dragged Munin from his back to cut down savagely on top of the skull of another. Munin split the falling man's head like a knife cutting through warm bread. Blood spattered Hundr's face and flowed down his hand in a hot, gory rush. He twisted Soulstealer free and charged forwards expecting to meet another enemy, but there was only blue sky and a grey stallion cropping at the grass beyond the battle.

He had punched through the whole Frankish line, and he laughed with the joy of breaking their feeble shield wall. He spun around and saw that where he cleft the enemy line, Kolo and Haesten filled that gap with death and slaughter. So they'd split the Franks into two forces and were quickly becoming surrounded. Hundr heard a roar further up the line and saw the white plume of Bjorn's helmet flying in the wind, but he was surrounded by blades, and a huge man, as big as Bjorn himself, hacked at the son of Ragnar with a long sword. Hundr charged towards Bjorn, ducking under a spear thrust. He drove his blade through the back of one of Bjorn's attackers, the resistance of the man's body giving way as the sword tip punched through his chest. He shoved that screaming enemy forward and yanked on the blade, but she was trapped in the dying Frank's rib cage. Hundr cursed and let the blade go, instead cutting Soulstealer across the throat of a Frank who turned to meet his attack.

Bjorn looked at Hundr and grinned through his bear-like beard, the whites of his eyes luminous amidst the dark coating of blood on his helmet, face, and beard. As the attackers fell away to meet Hundr's attack, Bjorn squared off against the giant Frank, and the two exchanged blows in the blur of steel and weapon skill. Hundr swayed away from an axe meant for his face and took a step backwards from the three enemies who cut and jabbed at his body and face, Hundr barely able to parry and dodge away from their wicked edges. A roar came from his left, his blind side where his missing eye could not see, and Kolo charged into the three enemies, clearing them out like a bull stomping through a field of lambs. Ahead of Hundr, Bjorn had fallen to one knee and looked poised to meet Odin in Valhalla, but Hundr sprang forward and lunged with Munin to block the downward stroke of the Frankish blade. The power in the stroke drove Hundr into the blood-churned earth, and he rose to a crouch, waiting for the follow-up blow from the giant. But no blow came. The huge Frank was retreating down the hillside, urged on by his surviving men. The Vikings roared their victory, and Bjorn Ironside grabbed Hundr in a huge embrace and lifted him from the ground. He dropped him and looked deep into Hundr's eye from the depths of his war helmet.

"That was Robert the Strong, and he would have sent me to Valhalla, but for your blade."

Hundr watched the Franks run down the hill, tripping and dropping weapons to escape the slaughter as quickly as possible. He had saved the life of one son of Ragnar, and another wanted to take his head. The army would rest for the afternoon following their victory on that blood-soaked hill, which left Hundr with three days before he could get back to the Seaworm.

TEN

The battle on the hill had lasted only moments, and the Vikings were victorious, having only sustained a handful of casualties. Hundr had supposed they would rest following the engagement, but Haesten gave the order to march on immediately. His army was deep inside Frankia, and with the collapse of Robert the Strong's army, the country opened up before them. The afternoon sun waned, and a greyness tinted the clouds as they marched through a deep valley and came within sight of a walled town; a Christ Church soared above all the other buildings with a high narrow gable and a cross facing toward the Viking's approach. The city walls were stout and well-made of stone-washed white, and the golden thatch of its buildings was visible above those walls like sheaves of wheat gathered in the harvest.

The town burghers had scuttled out of the

gates at the approach of the army, with Haesten and Bjorn meeting them for a brief discussion. The burghers nodded and bowed vigorously, and they wisely opened the town gates without a fight.

Hundr sat on a bench in the high beamed hall of the Church, where he and Kolo shared pots of ale and ate heartily of the food provided by the townspeople. The higher-ranking warriors of the army had taken up residence in the Church, with the main body of Haesten and Bjorn's army gathered in the town square to enjoy the spoils of victory.

"The ale is good, no?" said Kolo with a wide smile, the froth from his ale cup gathering on the shining black hairs of his moustache. Hundr nodded. It was good ale. The townspeople had made piles of ale, food, and gold, silver, and iron at the centre of the market square, which the Vikings now enjoyed.

"The townspeople are wise," said Hundr, "to not give up their lives for their possessions."

"Their soldiers were defeated. There cannot be many warriors here. It was a good decision. Better this way than to storm the walls every time we capture a town, my friend."

"Is it always this way with Haesten?"

"He learned the hard way down South. Better to win a battle, then negotiate for what we want.

We only have so many warriors, difficult to re-place, and storming walls is grim business, my friend. Many die on the walls where even a child or grandmother can hurl a rock down to crush a man's skull on the climb."

Hundr knew that was true. It was the great weakness of Viking armies that they had finite numbers. They only had the men their ships could carry. If too many of those men were lost, then the campaign was over. There had to be enough warriors left to crew the ships should they wish to leave, and they could not replace men until the following Spring brought a new season of campaigning. So whilst Vikings had a well-deserved reputation for ferocity and fight-ing skill, they were also cautious, and campaigns needed to be well planned.

"So that's why we attacked them uphill," said Hundr.

"Better that than climbing the walls."

"Give me an uphill battle against those tiny shields any day." A shiver ran down Hundr's spine, and he shuddered, recalling the horror of climbing the walls at Yorvik. Dragging himself up a ladder slick with blood and up into blades, rocks, and fire. He had fought back to back with Ivar that day and earned an arm ring from the son of Ragnar for his exploits.

They both laughed at that truth, but it sur-

113

prised Hundr at how easily they had defeated the Franks. Their shields were much smaller than the Viking equivalents, and they could not stand against the tactics of the Viking shield wall.

"They don't use the shield wall, these Franks," said Hundr, and Kolo shook his head.

"No, they seem to think spears and arrows will win battles. It was the same in the South, with the Muslim men."

"Muslim men?" Hundr had heard of such people before. He had seen their coins with strange curved writing. Their silver was of excellent quality and prized amongst traders.

"Yes, the men who sold me to Haesten. They were no match for the shield wall either."

"They look like you, these Muslim men?"

"No, they are from further East, my friend. Their Empire is vast. They make you Vikings look like children."

Hundr laughed, "Children?"

"Yes, they have better buildings, better weapons, bigger armies. They are very clever."

"Were you taken from your family?"

Kolo's smile faded, and he stared at the rushes on the Church floor. "I was only a boy when I was taken by a rival tribe. They killed my people and took us north. Sold the children and women to the Muslim men."

"Do you miss your home?"

Kolo shook his head, and a wan smile drooped across his normally cheerful face.

"It is very far away, too far. I will never see it again. None of your people will ever travel that far south, my friend. What about your home?" Kolo said, and he drank deep from his ale then took a deep breath to calm himself. He breathed out slowly, and Kolo's shoulders relaxed, as though with that breath he could suppress those memories of his faraway home. Hundr thought it must be far away indeed for men to have skin so much darker than the people of the north.

"My home is in the East," said Hundr.

"Do you miss your home?"

Hundr hadn't thought of his home for months. He had been so caught up with the pain and suffering of all that had happened to him in Northumbria that he hadn't given his old life any thought at all.

"It was not a happy place," Hundr said quietly.

"You are a Jarl, no? You must have been wealthy, brought up well?"

Hundr recalled himself as a boy, running through the laneways and alleys of his father's great city. Novgorod was a vast place, far beyond anything Hundr had seen in England or Frankia.

115

"I was not my father's first son." Hundr was a bastard, his mother a concubine. His father had legitimate sons from his wives, and Hundr was on the outside of that inner circle. But, his father had allowed Hundr access to the same masters as his other sons, and so Hundr had been well trained in weapons, strategy, and lore.

"Ah," said Kolo, nodding slowly. "Well, you have done well in life, no? You are a Jarl. I know you lost a ship, but you fight well, and after this victory, you are rich again, my friend." Kolo laughed, throwing his head back. His laughter echoed around the high church walls.

"Do you ever wonder what your life would have been like had your tribe not been defeated and you were a free man?"

Kolo shrugged and waved his hand at Hundr. "I do not think of such things. I have travelled far beyond lands any of my people have ever seen before. Haesten treats me well. I do not live like a slave. My life does not differ from any other Carl of his army."

Haesten did indeed treat Kolo well. He held a position of honour amongst Haesten's personal guard, and as much freedom as any other man. Kolo fought well, and Hundr had seen the Franks flinch at Kolo's strange appearance, and so he was a valuable warrior. Hundr thought of himself when he had run away from Novgorod. He'd fled, wanting to prove himself in the world. His only plan was to join a Viking raiding crew somewhere and become a drengr, a warrior with a reputation. His dream was to return to Novgorod with a warrior's reputation and show his father how wrong he had been to rebuke and deny him. Hundr drained his ale. That dream became lost when he met Saoirse in Northumbria. That doomed love crushed his dream of reputation and glory, and had ultimately led him to where he was now. *I must forget her and Sten. Maybe the way is East, get rich and go home.*

"How are your wounds?" said Hundr.

Kolo stretched his torso and groaned. "They are not too bad. I will live. You could have killed me. I won't forget that you spared my life, my friend. How did you come by that?" Kolo pointed to Hundr's missing eye.

Hundr raised his hand and allowed his fingers to brush over his ravaged face, the pain of the wounds flashing through his skull still a vivid memory.

"I fought in England and was captured. A man cut me and took my eye. I loved his woman, and he wanted me to suffer."

"A woman? Was she beautiful?"

"She was. I would have died for her."

"There must be some women in this town.

Come, let's go outside and see," said Kolo, and he slapped Hundr on the thigh. They rose and walked to the wide oak doors of the church and emerged into a throng of singing and laughing, with Bjorn Ironside at the centre capering from one foot to the other. He held a huge horn of ale in one hand whose contents were slopping in every direction as he danced and shouted with his men.

On the march from the battlefield to the town, Hundr had fallen in with Jarl Arne, who had explained that these lands belonged to the Frankish King, Charles the Bald, and that Robert the Strong commanded this region on Charles's behalf. The country was called Anjou, or Maine. Arne wasn't sure. What Arne did know, and the grin beneath his red beard was a testament to the fact, was this was only one town of many which now lay unprotected ahead of the Viking advance, and there were Cities to be taken too, cities full of rich churches and overflowing with silver.

Hundr saw the truth in Arne's words beyond, where Bjorn drank and danced with his men. There was a steady line of Frankish townspeople walking to place their valuables, silver, and gold trinkets on the back of a cart which was filling fast with candlesticks, ornate plates, and brooches.

"There he is!" boomed Bjorn's voice over the

crowd. "This man saved my life. Get out of my way," he said, barging through the warriors, showering them in whatever ale remained in his horn.

He clasped Hundr in another bear hug and laughed, smothering Hundr with spittle and his foul ale breath. *One day, he will break my ribs with these hugs.*

"Jarl... what's your name? Doesn't matter. You need ale, get him ale! Are you wounded? Doesn't matter either," said Bjorn, and laughed again.

"Kolo, I hear he bested you. No mean feat. Kolo is almost as strong as me. We will wrestle later, Kolo," said Bjorn.

A grinning warrior handed Hundr a pot of ale, which he took and thanked the man.

"I owe you now," said Bjorn. "Ask anything of me, anything at all."

Hundr thought about that. *I should ask him to help me kill his brother.* What he really needed to do was get back to the Seaworm. There were three days left until he must meet Einar back at the river on the Frankish coast, and it would take at least one full day to get there given how far Hundr had travelled inland and away from that point in the river. His plan was to simply sneak away and travel back to the place where he had jumped ship. The key problem with that plan was there was still no sign of Ivar the Boneless.

It was surprising that Ivar had not come across his brother's ships in the river and joined up with him.

"I came with a ship, which was lost, but my other ship will be here soon. I need men to ride with me to meet my warriors," said Hundr. Bjorn pointed at one of his men, who had fallen over in his drunken state.

"Did you see that," Bjorn said, clapping Hundr on the shoulder, "can't handle his ale, bloody fool," he laughed raucously again. "What did you say?"

"You asked me to ask anything of you," said Hundr.

"Yes, yes anything."

"So, I asked for a few men to go with me to meet my ship." Hundr leaned around to see what had distracted Bjorn again. He looked across to where two men were shoving each other in some dispute close to the treasure cart. Erik, Haesten's brother, was there overseeing the loading of the cart, and it looked to be one of his men and one of Bjorn's men who had fallen out.

"Hold this," Bjorn said and thrust his empty ale horn into Hundr's hand. Bjorn set off through the crowd, hurling men out of his way, marching to their scene of the disagreement. He reached the men and punched his own man in the stomach, throwing him five paces across the square, then he grabbed Erik's man around the neck, swiped a pot of ale from a nearby warrior, and forced it into Erik's man's hand. The warriors around roared with laughter, and the confrontation was over. Bjorn went to speak quietly to Erik and then strode back towards the square.

"He's as strong as a bull," said Kolo.

"He's bloody mad," said Hundr. "Is he simple?" It seemed to Hundr that Bjorn was all bluster and brutal warrior comradery. He fought well. He had helped win the day in the battle with the Franks, and Bjorn had marched fearlessly into the hail of enemy arrows. From what Hundr had seen so far, however, this son of Ragnar lacked the guile of his savage brothers, whom Hundr had seen in Northumbria.

"Don't let him fool you. He's as sharp as a brooch pin that one," said Kolo.

"Kolo, Kolo," Bjorn was bellowing across the square. "Come here and wrestle with me. I'll have you this time, you big bastard."

Kolo grinned and made his way down to face Bjorn. The crowd of warriors separated to give the men space. Kolo and Bjorn circled each other for a few moments and then launched at each other. Their chests smashed together like great prize bulls, and they scrambled at each other's limbs for hold.

Whilst the wrestling match went on and the

warriors cheered, Hundr felt a tap on his shoulder. He spun around to see Erik standing behind him, snow-white eyebrows frowning as usual.

"Bjorn told me to lend you five men," he said.

Hundr rocked with surprise. He hadn't thought Bjorn was listening.

"Yes, I need to meet my other ship with the rest of my men."

"You never mentioned that before."

"They are only due to arrive now. They were delayed leaving England."

"I'll go with you. We leave in the morning at first light." said Erik, and spun on his heel.

Hundr scratched at his dead eye, the scar on his face itched, and the hollow of his eye throbbed. Soon he would get to meet Einar and his crew, and now he could travel safely. But if Erik was going with him and they bumped into Ivar, it could still mean death. *How would I explain that situation away?* Also, he had to get to Einar first to make sure the crew knew who Jarl Rune was. Things were going well. Hundr would have his share of the town's plunder, and he was relatively safe from Ivar for now. He would be on his way to meet the Seaworm, but it all dangled on a knife's edge. If Ivar turned up, it could still mean death, and if the Seaworm crew gave away his lie, this new opportunity for wealth with Haesten and

Bjorn could quickly turn into capture and pain.

ELEVEN

Six men rode with Hundr through the fields
and woods of the Frankish countryside. Erik and
four of his men made the journey, and Kolo had
insisted on coming along. Haesten's army had a
string of captured horses, and they had provided
Hundr with a piebald gelding. Riding on a com-
pliant horse, astride a comfortable saddle, was
very different to the journey he had made in the
opposite direction, riding without a saddle on an
old plough mare.

The band was well provisioned with ale and
food. Erik's men carried sacks of cheese, bread,
and meat. There were frequent stops for re-
freshment, which lasted rather longer than they
would if the journey were urgent, but Hundr
didn't complain. With a day to spare before he
was to meet Einar, he enjoyed Kolo's company, so
it suited him to take the journey in a relaxed way,
laughing and joking with his new friend. There

had been precious little laughter in Hundr's life, especially since his ordeal in Northumbria, and so the journey across Frankia made him feel lighter. All Kolo wanted to talk about was the countryside and how different it was from his homeland. He talked of the strange animals in his lands, enormous beasts who roamed the plains and dense forests. Kolo talked of pets and weapons he had loved and lost. It was simple talk, which Hundr enjoyed. Erik and his men kept to themselves. They rode twenty paces behind Hundr and Kolo but were generous with their food and ale.

They arrived at the riverbank where Hundr had killed two of Ivar's men on the sand the evening before Einar was due to arrive. The wooded island where the Seaworm had turned and fled from Ivar's wrath was there in the centre of the widening river. He glanced up and down the length of the river, dreading to see Ivar's two black sails with the feared white Raven banner etched on the sailcloth, but Ivar was nowhere to be seen.

"Your ship must be close by then?" said Erik, who had joined Hundr on the river bank.

"Yes, it's downstream. It might still be here, beyond that bend."

"Why would it not be there?"

"Franks could have taken it. Anyone could have

taken it. It's a ship. You would have to have a lucky summer raiding to have enough silver to buy a ship like that."

"How does your other ship know to meet you here, at this spot?" Erik tipped his head back and looked along his nose at Hundr. Haesten's brother didn't believe his story, that was clear, and he hadn't warmed to Hundr at all. Hundr supposed that in fairness to Erik, he was right not to believe him because he was lying. But Bjorn and Kolo had welcomed Hundr to a certain extent, and he felt more a part of this army than he had in Northumbria. Haesten kept to himself, and Hundr had rarely seen him, but the rest of the men were welcoming.

"They pursued us up this river. I could call across the bows to my other ship to sail around that island and back to the sea. Then meet me here if anything went wrong."

"Why didn't you fight? You had two ships of warriors?"

"Enough questions, my friends. Come, let's eat what's left of the food and drink what's left of the ale," said Kolo, draping his heavy muscled arms across Hundr and Erik's shoulders.

Kolo had saved Hundr from Erik's probing, but if he couldn't get to Einar before Erik questioned him further, then the ruse would be up.

The Seaworm arrived as Hundr knew she

would, turning around the distant bend in the estuary and ambling against the tide with long, slow oar strokes. The sun caught the drips of river water from her oar blades, making them glisten like jewels. Hundr, waited atop the sandbank he had climbed days earlier. He tried to maintain an air of calm, but his heart was in his mouth. If Bush or Blink or one of the others called his name as the ship approached, then the game could well be up, and they would expose Jarl Rune as a fraud. Hundr supposed he could always put his knife in Erik's belly and wade out to the Seaworm to sail off into the wide sea, but Erik's men would cut him down before he was even knee-deep in the water.

Einar stood tall at the steerboard and raised a hand to Hundr as the ship drew close. He waved in return and smiled to see Ragnhild leaning over the sheer strake. Erik came to stand alongside him.

"A fine ship," he said, tucking his hands into his belt.

"The finest. The Seaworm is her name."

Hundr risked a sideways glance at Erik with his good eye, and the white-haired warrior licked his lips and clenched his jaw. Hundr knew Erik was impatient to get to question the crew, and he wondered why Erik wanted so badly to prove that he was lying? What difference did it make to Erik who Hundr was? He had not fought for Haesten and had saved Bjorn's life? *Perhaps he is jealous. Maybe he wants a bigger standing for himself amongst the army. Or maybe he just wants trouble.*

Hundr looked back towards Kolo, and the big man nodded his head in appreciation of the ship's quality. Erik glanced back to see what Hundr looked at, which was his intention all along, and whilst Erik was distracted, Hundr ran down the sandbank and into the river. He waded into the water towards the ship, almost sensing Erik's fury at being outwitted. The Seaworm drew in her oars and glided towards the shore, coming to a stop just ahead of where Hundr waded towards them. Ragnhild dropped a seal-hide rope ladder over the side and extended her hand to help him up.

"Ragnhild," Hundr hissed as he struggled through the water, "you must call me Jarl Rune. Jarl Rune- tell the others quickly."

She shook her head, grinning at his scheming, and leaned further over the side to hear him better, but he couldn't talk any louder, or Erik would hear him. Hundr cursed and got a hand on the ladder, and hauled himself up.

"Hundr, good to see alive," shouted Brownlegs, joining Ragnhild to peer down at him. Hundr sighed and cursed to himself.

"Hundr, you wily dog," said Bush from somewhere amidships.

Hundr climbed the ladder, where Ragnhild and Brownlegs hauled him over the side. He thudded onto the deck and pulled Brownlegs and Ragnhild down towards him.

"Call me Jarl Rune. I'll explain later. Tell the others, quickly," he said. Ragnhild nodded and hurried towards Einar. Brownlegs was staring at him, slack-jawed and frowning. "I'll explain later."

Hundr stood and waved over to Erik and Kolo.

"My other ship is beyond the next bend," he shouted to Erik. "We will meet you there. Kolo, why don't you come with us?"

Erik nodded and returned to his men, and Kolo waded into the water and climbed up to Hundr aboard the Seaworm. As he clambered over the side, Brownlegs and Hrist gasped at his appearance, and Kolo laughed. Hundr allowed himself to laugh along, despite the awkward position in which he now found himself with Erik. Haesten's brother would surely have noticed that the crew did not address Hundr as "Jarl" and called him Hundr. Yet he laughed now because he had forgotten Kolo looked so different from anyone the crew would have seen before, they would never have seen a man from so far south, and Kolo's monstrous size combined with the unusual hue

129

of his skin made him terrifying to look upon for the first time. Guthmund, Hrorik, and Hjalmar clutched at their hammer pendants and whispered together, staring wide-eyed at Kolo.

"This is my friend, Kolo," Hundr said and introduced Kolo to each of the Seaworm crew. "He fights like a demon, and he has my trust."

"What kind of Loki spawn do you bring onto the ship?" hissed Guthmund, and the newer crew members nodded vigorously and shuffled in behind Guthmund.

"I said he is my friend. If you have a problem, you are welcome to fight him, Guthmund," Hundr said. Guthmund looked at Kolo, and then his face flushed red behind his grizzled beard, and he cast his eyes down to the deck. Kolo laughed in a low rumble, and Hundr smiled.

Einar ordered the crew to lower the oars, and the ship came about. Erik and his men rode off slowly towards the bend in the river. Hundr allowed himself a little smile that he had got to the crew before Erik, even if he had heard them address him as Hundr. Bringing Kolo aboard would help cover the ruse.

"You're still alive then," said Ragnhild, and she smiled, which looked odd on her scarred face, usually so serious.

"Just about. Listen, and I'll explain later, but you and the crew must call me Jarl Rune."

130

"I'm not calling you Jarl, you jumped up…"

"Ragnhild, trust me," Hundr said and placed his hand on her shoulder. She looked at his hand and back at him, her face restored to its usual frown. "I had to say the ship we attacked was mine. I am with Jarl Haesten now. Tell the others."

She shook his hand off and nodded. She went to talk to Hrist, and Hundr made his way across the bilge towards the steerboard where Einar stood with his hand on the tiller. Hildr was with him.

"I see you have made some strange friends," said Einar, nodding towards Kolo, who had taken a place on a bench and grabbed an oar to help get the ship moving.

"He's a good man and a fine warrior. Einar, what I am going to say is even stranger than my new friend. But you and the crew must call me Jarl Rune. I've fallen in with Jarl Haesten, and there is all the silver you will ever need at our fingertips. But to get it, you must call me Jarl until we leave." Hundr watched Einar's head tilt to one side, and he scratched at his beard. Einar looked at Hildr, who shrugged.

"Who says we want to go with Jarl Haesten? We agreed to go North," said Einar.

"Einar, trust me. We don't have a choice. Have you seen Ivar?"

"No, not a sign of him. But we saw a fleet of Ragnarsson ships enter the river. We can just drop your friend here over the side, turn around, and sail away. We don't have to go to Jarl Haesten," Einar said.

Hundr sighed. Einar was right. They could drop Kolo over the side and sail away. It would be simple to bring the Seaworm about, sail around the island in the same way Einar had days earlier, and be off out on the open sea. But Einar had not seen what Hundr had seen. They were deep into Frankia, into territory not raided by Northmen before. The Franks fought bravely, but their shield wall was no match for Viking skill and tactics. There was silver there for the taking and an opportunity to make themselves rich.

"Einar, trust me. There is enough silver here to buy you all the land you want. We can join Haesten, get rich, and sail away with enough silver to properly crew the Seaworm and buy you land. Then we can take Ragnhild, Hildr, and Hrist back to Upsala and find you a woman." As he said those last words, Hundr noticed Einar and Hildr exchange a glance and then quickly look away from each other.

"What about the Ragnarsson fleet?" said Einar. "We are past the island now. Let's just bring her about and be off, lad."

"It's Bjorn Ironside. He's allied to Haesten."

"Bjorn bloody Ironside," said Einar and laughed.

THE WRATH OF IVAR

"You mean Ivar's brother Bjorn Ironside?"

"Yes, but Ivar is not there. They think I am a Jarl who was attacked and lost his ship in this river. Einar, if we do this right, we can sail the ship we attacked upriver, join Haesten, fight a few easy skirmishes, and get out of here rich and with two ships. Simple. Two ships for you to command, Einar."

The old Jarl frowned at Hundr and scratched at his beard again.

"You know what Simple did, don't you?" Einar asked. Hundr shook his head.

"No, Einar, I don't know what Simple did. Are you with me on this or not?"

"Simple followed a shit cart and thought it was a wedding."

"What's that supposed to mean?"

"Nothing is simple. Ivar is around here some-where baying for our blood. Bjorn Ironside is here with a whole bloody fleet, and you want us to sail into that to kill some Franks for a man we don't even know. We swore we would never serve another man again, that we would be masters of our own destiny."

"We did, and we don't have to swear to Haes-ten. He doesn't want our oaths. He is fighting for a Frankish Duke in a land dispute, and he just wants to get rich. Like us. Let's get what we're due, Einar. We can't just keep sailing up and down the coast with half a crew and no plan."

Einar looked at Hildr again, and she shrugged. "Why not do what we're good at? Get you your silver and get out," she said. *You can always bank on a Valkyrie to run towards the fight.*

"Very well. Let's go to Haesten and right back into the bloody hornets' nest," said Einar. With a huff, he threw his hands up and went to the tiller.

Hundr grinned and clapped his friend on the shoulder. A plan was forming in Hundr's mind. He watched Kolo pull at his oar, the big warrior already laughing and joking with Bush, Brownlegs, and Blink. If it were still there, they could reclaim the ship they had left for dead upriver and sail to Haesten, fight Duke Salomon's war, get rich, and sail away with two ships and two bilges full of silver. He would fight under Jarl Rune's name and not his own, but Hundr was not his name either. He pictured himself sailing into Novgorod. Velmud the bastard, returned as the owner of two ships with two crews at his back, ships sitting low in the water because they were so full of treasure. Einar could have his land wherever he wanted. Ragnhild, Hildr, and Hrist would be back in Upsala at Odin's temple, and he could return to his father with the reputation and glory he had always dreamed of. He pictured the look on his father's face, and all the other noblemen of Novgorod, when he marched into the city like a hero. He smiled to himself. It would be so easy. All the troubles of Northumbria, Saoirse, and Sten would be behind him, and he would leave Frankia rich and powerful.

TWELVE

Einar leant on his shield and traced the fine carvings around the rim of his helmet. It was a beautiful thing, made by Frankish smiths reputed to be the finest in the world. It had a conical top and a rim around the edge carved with markings Einar didn't understand. They weren't the runes of his homeland, and Hundr's friend Kolo had assured Einar it was the writing of the Romans. Einar didn't care. It was worth a fortune. It had a nasal guard and a hard strip of leather fixed to the back to protect his neck.

He had to concede that Hundr was right about the rich pickings to be had in this war, a war whose true purpose was difficult to understand. Haesten and Bjorn had welcomed them. Bjorn's welcome boisterous and genuine, where Haesten's was dismissive but not hostile. Bjorn was older than Einar and of a similar age to Ivar. Einar had grown up on Ivar's estates, and it had in fact been Ivar who had first named him Rosti, the Brawler. Einar remembered Bjorn coming to visit, and he was then as he was now, full of life and laughter and loved by all. Bjorn had no memory of Einar. He had been but a pup back then. So, luckily, Hundr's story of Jarl Rune had not been questioned. Kolo had noticed that the crew called Hundr by that name, and not Jarl Rune, but many Northmen went by nicknames, including most of the Seaworm crew, and so they passed it off in that way. Yet Erik was still suspicious of Hundr and was keeping a careful eye upon him.

Einar stood in line with Hundr on one side and Ragnhild on the other. On the other side of Hundr, Kolo, the giant, black-skinned warrior, stood spear in hand and staring at the high Roman walls before them. They all waited for the order to advance. Haesten had brought the army to the largest city in the region, Le Mans he heard it called. They had raided across wide swathes of Anjou, Touraine, and now Maine, encountering barely any organised resistance. It all seemed too good to be true, and Einar wondered if there was an enormous force of Franks waiting beyond those high Roman walls waiting to unleash their vengeance for the weeks of raiding, for the lost towns and butchered menfolk.

He placed the helmet on and enjoyed how snugly it fitted his skull, almost as though it had been made for him. Some men hated to fight with a helmet on. Hundr and Sten both disliked the way it reduced vision and awareness. Einar had taken this piece of armour from a Lord's hall in a town they'd sacked a week earlier. It would protect him from any blows or rocks coming from the walls as he scaled the ladders of Le Mans. His guts twisted at the thought, and Einar shifted his feet. He had assaulted cities before, Yorvik being the most recent. He had climbed the ladder on that day of blood and death, climbing each rung and wanting to cry out with terror as men around him fell to the earth pierced by spear or slashed by axe, or heads caved in by rocks thrown from the battlements. Einar swallowed, but his mouth was dry, and his throat felt like the bottom of a grain sack.

"How is it?" Hundr asked, pointing at Einar's belly.

"Fine, it won't hold me back." It wasn't fine, though. It hurt. Even thinking about the wound in his guts brought back the feeling of Ivar's blade inside him. It had not, however, been the blade that caused the most pain. It had been the days and months afterwards. Hildr and Hrist had tended the wound, and there was no one who could have done a better job, but Einar had been curled up into a ball of writhing agony - sweating with fever, the burning of the hole deep inside him unbearable and crippling. Hildr told him afterwards that he'd cried for his mother, a woman he barely remembered, she having died when Einar was a small child.

"I know," Hundr replied. Einar turned and nodded at Ragnhild. She winked her one eye at him and adjusted the strap of her shield. He leant around Ragnhild to see Hildr. She saw him too and smiled. Einar smiled back, and the sight of her lifted his heart. She had tended to him through the long months of sickness. He was sure that without Hildr and Hrist and their Valkyrie healing skills, he would have died screaming without a blade in his hand, writhing in the bilge of the Seaworm. Hildr stood battle-ready, axe in one hand and shield in another. She had long golden hair, she was broad in the shoulder and hip, and she fought with a fury few could match. Hildr had blue eyes, which on the battlefield looked as cold as ice, but Einar saw only warmth there. She was a fine woman, a woman to be admired. They had grown close, and as Einar had healed and could stand, they talked together. Sometimes they would wait until the crew were asleep and would walk along on the deck of the Seaworm, listening to the gentle sounds of the sea, and gazing upon the heavens. Einar wasn't sure if she wanted to return to the Valkyrie temple at Upsala with Ragnhild. He hadn't asked her for fear that she might say she did.

A horn blew from towards the front lines, and

Einar could see the head of Bjorn Ironside in the distance, marching up and down the Viking lines shouting words of encouragement, but Einar couldn't hear them.

"Make ready, we go in the third wave," Hundr said, and Einar nodded. It wasn't so long ago that he gave the orders, Einar the Brawler, Ivar the Boneless' trusted Jarl and dog of war. He wasn't interested in that anymore. Deep down in the cavernous pit of his belly wound, Einar wanted peace. Down in the depths of his fever and tears, he thought his fighting days were over. He hadn't had to raise a blade in anger since the day he had fought Ivar. The skirmishes in Frankia happened around him, and when they had taken the Viking ship weeks earlier in that Frankish river, he hadn't needed to strike a blow. The fighting all happened too quickly.

The front lines made the shield wall and marched towards the walls of Le Mans. As they marched, the warriors chanted a war song that rang out across the battlefield.

"We fight with swords,

We hold bloody shields,

We stain our spears,

Showers of arrows break the shields into pieces,

Prepare yourselves, for here we come."

The battle song stirred in Einar's chest, and he

tightened his grip on his shield. Arrows poured down from the city walls but mostly thudding harmlessly into the advancing shield wall or skitting off the surface of shields to fly away. The barrage of arrows was not as heavy as Einar expected, which he hoped meant they did not heavily defend the city. There had been some talk of the city opening its gates, like most of the towns in the region had, to avoid a slaughter. But the city rulers of Le Mans decided to fight. So Einar must go up the ladders, and the people inside the city would die.

The front rank stopped its advance, and ladders were lifted and placed against the walls. Archers raced forward from the second rank and peppered the battlements with shafts to stop the defenders from throwing the ladders away, and with a roar, the front rankers began their climb. Einar's guts clenched again as he watched those brave men race up the ladders. They were doing so on a promise of arm rings and silver and reputation, driving for the honour of being first over the wall. But then came the rocks and arrows, and the screaming started. More men began their climb until the ladders were thick with Vikings, climbing the walls like lines of ants on a summer's day. A huge cauldron appeared at the wall's summit, and the defenders poured a thick, black, steaming substance over the attackers. Pitchers of oil, Einar assumed. An archer lent between the crenulation in the wall and shot a flaming arrow into the scalded warriors. There was a spark, and ten men burst into flames, flailing their arms and screaming like nothing Einar had ever heard before. Those men fell to the ground writhing in agony. Einar closed his eyes tight, his breath coming in short sharp bursts and his chest heaving. It would be his turn soon, and he hadn't lifted a blade since his fight with Ivar, where he had suffered the grievous wound that did not kill.

They shuffled forwards, and ahead men leaped over the battlements. Einar hoped the doors would be pushed open soon and he wouldn't need to make the climb. *Why am I thinking like this? I am Einar Rosti, lover of battle and a man of reputation.* He took a deep breath to steady himself. He looked to Hundr, who was grinning at Kolo, the excitement of the battle to come etched onto his ravaged face, one eye blazing with anticipation. Before his wound, Einar would have felt the same, but today was different. He wasn't thinking of striking a blow, of furthering his reputation amongst the warriors. Einar wanted to hang back, let the others go up and win the glory. He felt ashamed of himself like he needed to jump into a river and scrub his skin clean of these un-warrior-like thoughts. He looked at Hildr, and she smiled at him again. Einar hoped she didn't have to go up the wall. A vision of her

lying in the dirt and screaming from a horren-
dous wound filled his mind's eye, and he nearly
vomited.

Einar felt heat on his face, and suddenly they
were there at the ladders. The burning corpses
were still aflame, the stink of the burning flesh
filling his nostrils. Einar glanced up to see the
enormous figure of Bjorn Ironside on the wall's
summit, laying about him with an axe and
bellowing in defiance at the city's defenders. He
swallowed as it became his turn to make the
climb. Einar reached out his hand and recoiled
from the thick blood dripping from the rung.
Einar cursed himself. He had done this many
times; always he was the first, the most reckless
of his own safety. A shoulder barged him out of
the way, and he turned as Hundr grabbed the
ladder and hurtled up the rungs, Kolo on the opposite ladder as the two friends raced to the top.
A spear flashed over the battlements, and Hundr
swung aside, narrowly avoiding its point, and it
slammed into the ground at Einar's feet. Next,
Ragnhild pushed in front of him, holding her
axe haft between her teeth and flying up behind
Hundr.

A groaning, creaking sound came from Einar's
left, and his heart lifted as Le Mans' wide timber gates slowly opened. From that entranceway
strode Haesten, his face and fish scale Brynjar
splashed with blood and gore. The Jarl roared

and waved at the rest of his army, and Einar laughed. He threw his head back and laughed with relief. Then shame washed over him. He shouldn't be feeling relief, it should disappoint him to not have struck a blow. Hildr was next to him, filling the space made by Ragnhild. Their shoulders were touching, and he reached out and subtly grabbed her hand. It was warm and welcoming, and she squeezed his fingers. He looked down into her blue eyes, and as the last assault on his bravery, he thought he would cry. Einar fought back the tears of relief. She was unhurt and had not made the climb. He wanted to hold her close, but he did not. Instead, his heart despaired for his lost courage and love of battle, but the space made by that lost courage was filled with love for Hildr, she who had sewn his guts together and saved his life.

Once the gates were open, the city fell as easily as a child's sandcastle when the tide came in. The place had not been well defended, only fifty Frankish warriors had manned the walls, the rest of the defenders had been mere townspeople. Bakers, tanners, merchants, all fighting bravely but poorly to protect their city. Le Mans' Lords had given her up to the Viking attackers. Robert the Strong had not wanted to waste his warriors in the defence of these people. The city contained a huge cathedral, as the Christ Priests called it, a monstrous building devoted to their god, and which was filled with silver plate and candlesticks. The priests' fingers were thick with rings, and their necks heavy with gold chains, and the Vikings laughed with glee as they gathered those spoils to be split amongst the warriors. He had to concede that Hundr was right. They were rich men now and about to become richer. Einar himself already wore two gold chains twisted around his neck and hanging against his mail, not to mention the silver they had accumulated from previous raids.

Hundr and Kolo ambled over to join Einar, and Kolo handed him a wineskin. Einar took a draught, and it was delicious, fruity, red, and silky pouring down his throat.

"You were right," Einar said, and Hundr smiled.

"I think you have enough wealth to buy your piece of land now, old friend," Hundr said.

Einar nodded. "Haesten and Bjorn are generous." And they were. They shared most of the treasure amongst their men, which kept them loyal and eliminated any kind of discord between the crews and Jarls.

"Most of these men have sailed the world with Haesten and Bjorn," said Kolo, "They have won and lost fortunes and won them again."

"Why does Haesten want his wealth?"

"More ships, my friend. He lost half his fleet in

the great storm near where they bought me from my old masters. Same for Bjorn. Sixty ships they had, and now only half that number."

Other Jarls came to join them where they sat. Arne and Knut nodded greetings to Hundr, and they spoke briefly of the battle and how poorly the Franks had defended the city.

"It makes me nervous," said Jarl Knut. "They must be out there, gathering an army where we can't see them."

"Aye," nodded Jarl Arne, scratching at his red beard. "We haven't seen Robert the Strong since he nearly killed Ironside on that hilltop."

They all nodded at the truth of that. Einar thought the same. Robert had sacrificed much of his lands to the Vikings, which was no simple decision. He must surely marshal his forces to strike hard and soon.

"I hear Duke Salomon is coming here to talk with Haesten," said Jarl Knut.

"We are all rich now, maybe this war is over for us, and we can leave the Franks to fight between themselves," said Arne. Einar nodded. He must talk to Hundr about that. They weren't sworn to Haesten or Bjorn, and they surely had enough silver now to leave this war and make the trip North. But as he watched Hundr talking and laughing with Kolo as the two shared their wine, he did not recall ever seeing the young war-

146

rior look so content, perhaps even happy. Hundr had suffered. He had made bad choices in Northumbria, pursuing Hakon Ivarsson's wife, and he bore the marks of those choices in the scars on his face and the weight of Sten's betrayal turned Hundr's heart into a stone. It would be hard to persuade Hundr to leave because Jarl Rune was a respected leader of Haesten and Bjorn's forces. Bjorn loved Hundr. The lad had saved his life, and they would march and drink and laugh together. It was easy to like Bjorn. Hundr had respect, wealth, and reputation, which were the things all Northmen craved and fought for. Einar knew now with certainty that his days of fighting and war were over. He didn't have the belly for it anymore. He had fought more Holmgang's than most warriors. Einar had assaulted cities and fought in countless shield walls. He had even gone toe to toe with the Champion of the North, Ivar the Boneless. Ivar's sword had taken the fight out of him, and he couldn't suffer the pain of that wound again. So he would go North and find some rest. He hoped Hildr would go with him and he would talk to Hundr. Perhaps he could put his time as a warrior behind him.

THIRTEEN

Two days after the capture of Le Mans, Duke Salomon arrived outside the city walls. Hundr was part of the group of Viking leaders who welcomed the Duke to the city, along with Haesten, Bjorn, Arne, and Knut. Salomon came at the head of a line of mounted warriors, all with good mail and swords at their hips, which was a testament to the wealth of the Frankish Kingdoms. Salomon was a tall thin man with a long-nosed face above a black beard streaked with patches of pure white. He wore a circlet of silver on his head, and to Hundr he looked like a King, or at least like a man who fancied himself a King.

Salomon slipped from his saddle and approached the line of Viking Jarls. Two of his warriors flanked him, big flat-faced men who looked vacantly at the city walls behind the Northmen. Salomon spoke in a high-pitched voice and in the language of the Franks, which Hundr did not understand. Even more surprising than Salomon's voice was that Haesten spoke back to him in Saloman's own language, and the Jarl spoke the words with confidence and ease.

The Duke waved his arm at the city and nodded his head in appreciation. He gestured behind him to a cart drawn by two horses, and Haesten waved its driver towards the city gates. Some more pleasantries were exchanged, and the delegation headed back towards the city. Hundr walked with Bjorn, who reeked of last night's ale.

"Looks like the Duke is happy," Bjorn said and closed one eye with a frown.

"Sore head, Lord?" asked Hundr.

"Too much ale last night. Ended up wrestling again."

"Did you win?"

"Of course I bloody won. I wasn't that drunk."

"Why is the Duke here?"

"Our arrangement was to defeat Robert the Strong and teach the Franks in these lands a lesson, soften them up a bit. We've done that," said Bjorn, and he winked at Hundr.

"So the war's over then?"

"Who knows? Old Salomon here wants to be a King. His land is Brittany, and he wants to rule that separately from the lands of the Franks."

"So he's not a Frank?"

"Sort of, but he's from Brittany. He wants the Frankish King Charles the Bald to recognise his position. Bloody silly name for a King, Charles the Bald."

"What do you mean?"

Bjorn huffed and threw up his arms. "Well, he could have picked Charles the Fierce, or Charles Blood Sword, or Charles Bear Killer."

Hundr laughed. "They are good names. Like yours, Lord."

"There'll be a feast tonight for the Duke. Then maybe we will leave."

"Have you got what you came for?"

"More than enough, enough to buy more ships and warriors to fill them."

"So, what will you do now?"

Bjorn stopped walking and looked at Hundr with one eyebrow raised. "Fight somewhere else. England maybe, or North, or go South again."

Hundr smiled, and Bjorn marched on. He wasn't surprised by what Bjorn said. It was the way all Northmen who chose the Viking path thought. All they wanted was reputation, wealth, and to earn a place in Valhalla. Hundr enjoyed that life, and as he watched Bjorn stroll through the city

and the men call out to him and wave greetings, he thought again about going home. Going
back to Novgorod had no guarantees. He had fled
the city to make his own life, and to forge his
own destiny. Hundr had dreamed of returning
in glory at the head of a pack of warriors and
dripping in silver, but his father may not even
care that he had left. He was just an inconveni-
ent bastard, and after his mother died, he had
barely seen his father at all. Hundr was sure that
if he asked, Bjorn would let him tag along on his
next adventure. There he would fight, drink ale,
find women, and be respected among the warriors as a man of reputation. *What more to life
is there?* He owed it to Einar and Ragnhild to
follow through on their wishes. He would help
Einar find his land and take Ragnhild, Hildr, and
Hrist back to Upsala. After that, though, maybe
he would not go East. The more he thought about
it, it was likely that his father would rebuke him
and send him away. The man had never shown
him any kindness, and why would that change
now? There was a burning inside of Hundr that
wanted his father to recognise his achievements,
for his father to respect him, but the more Hundr
thought about that, the less likely it seemed in
reality. He could, however, fulfil his promises
to Einar and Ragnhild, and then join up with
Bjorn again, to live life as Bjorn did, to live well
and with joy. Maybe Bush, Blink, and Brownlegs
would come with him. The only turd in that

water barrel of plans was Ivar. He was out there somewhere. He had disappeared up the river and was no doubt still searching for Hundr. Worse than that, he was Bjorn's brother. Bjorn would surely side with Ivar and turn Hundr over to him if it came to it. So, he had much to think about as the Northmen prepared for the feast with Duke Salomon.

The feast took place in Le Mans' town hall, in the western quarter of the city. It was a long building filled with benches, and at the centre of the space was a raised platform where the great Lords sat, ate, and congratulated each other on the successful campaign. At that top table sat Haesten, Bjorn, Erik, Knut, Arne, Salomon, and two of his men. They had asked Hundr to sit up there with them, which was a great honour, but he had asked instead for a table in the hall to drink and eat with his friends. And so, at a round table made of yellow-painted planks, he sat with Einar, Ragnhild, Kolo, Hildr, Hrist Bush, Blink, and Brownlegs. They dressed in whatever finery they could find in the city, which was a stark difference to the ragged, bloodstained clothing they had worn when first sailing up that wide Frankish river. Hundr wore a fine green tunic, leaving his precious Brynjar in his quarters hidden with his two swords behind the fireplace. He felt so much lighter without his war gear, and when he walked, he felt as light as a cloud. Even

Bush scrubbed up well, his bald patch covered with a merchant's piqued hat trimmed with fur. Hildr and Hrist both wore dresses, and the two fierce Valkyrie warriors looked just like normal women, if one ignored the scars on their faces and arms. Ragnhild refused to wear a dress, not that anyone had actually asked her to wear one. She sat there in her war gear, as serious and fierce as always.

"Take that bloody hat off," Brownlegs said to Bush and reached to grab at its tip.

"Leave it, eat your food, and stop breathing on me. Your breath smells like a sheep's arse," Bush replied, batting his hand away.

Hundr laughed, along with the rest of his friends. He raised his cup of ale, and the others all looked in his direction.

"A toast to all of us. It is not much more than a year since we sailed away from Northumbria. We had nothing then, and now look at us."

"I never thought to see so much silver," said Blink, grinning.

"We've barely had to lift our blades, not like the hard fighting in England," said Brownlegs.

Kolo drained his ale and belched, holding a hand up in apology. "I didn't mean to spoil the moment, my friend. Please, continue."

"Here's to new wealth and new friends," Hundr

said. The others raised their cups and drank their ale.

"To new friends," said Guthmund, echoing Hundr's toast. But the old crew did not raise their cups to that toast, and Guthmund's men just grumbled. Hundr saw Guthmund flash a sickly, brown-toothed grin in Einar's direction. The new men had still not bonded with the old, and Hundr knew he would need to remedy that if they were ever to form a proper crew.

"So, now we can get you your land," Hundr said, leaning across to look at Einar.

Einar nodded slowly and bit into a chunk of bread. Hundr noticed that Einar's gaze flitted to Hildr, and then back to him.

"Have you decided what you will do when this is over?" Einar said.

"It is time maybe to go home, east. Back to Novgorod. Then, who knows? I could throw in with Bjorn, maybe."

"What about Ivar?"

"What about him?"

"He won't give up hunting you, and Bjorn won't protect you from his brother."

Which was true, Hundr supposed. The most sensible thing was to take their two ships, try to get some more men to fill out the crews, and then head east and away from Ivar's reach. With two ships full of warriors, maybe he didn't have to run. He had faced Ivar before and could do so again. It was not the way of the drengr to run.

"Where will you look for land?" Hundr said. He didn't think Einar would warm to the idea of fighting Ivar. Einar was not the brutally violent man he had once been. Hundr had noticed that Einar had not fought when they took the ship in the river, nor had he shed blood in any of the Frankish towns or at Le Mans. No one could question Einar's bravery and reputation. He was a renowned fighter and had traded blows with the Boneless, but the terrible wound Ivar had inflicted upon Einar had undoubtedly taken its toll.

"I need to think it through," Einar said, looking into his cup of ale, "I would need to find somewhere where there is peace, and I would need warriors to help protect the land, and farmers to work it."

"We have enough silver now for all of that."

"We do. But I am not sure Bush and Blink and others would stay with me. They fear not going to Valhalla more than they want a peaceful life. Then there's the Seaworm."

"She is yours, Einar," Hundr said, but Einar bringing up the Seaworm, made Hundr's cheeks flush. He had assumed Einar would allow him to take the Seaworm to the east, or wherever he decided to go, but a ship was worth a fortune, and

Einar might not want to give her up.

"If my old crew wants to sail with you, then you can take her," Einar said, and he looked deep into Hundr's eye, and in those hard grey eyes, Hundr thought he saw a deep sadness.

"We have another ship Einar, you have done enough for me. You saved my life in Northumbria and suffered that awful wound for me."

"Aye." Einar stared at the table. The noise of Blink, Bush, and Kolo laughing and shouting at each other as they ate paled away. There was just Hundr and Einar now, locked in their own bond of friendship and loyalty.

"You decide what you want to do, Einar, and I will help you get it. We can always sail the Whale Road together again. Come east with me, see my city. There is opportunity there and land."

Einar looked at him and nodded again. "I don't know if I can fight anymore," he said, almost in a whisper, "the old fury, the old love for axe and shield and reputation, I think it bled out of me on that jetty and down Ivar's blade."

"You are as tough as..." Hundr said, but Einar held up a finger.

"I don't want to be a farmer, really. What do I know about land and farming? All I know is the axe and sea. I just want to settle down, have a quiet life, with a woman to hold." Einar looked at

Hildr again.

"You and Hildr have become close."

Einar smiled, and his flat slab face suddenly became open and warm. "She is an amazing woman. I could spend the rest of my days just looking at her."

Hundr clapped Einar on the back and raised his cup, downing the ale and shouting for more. "I am happy for you. She is a formidable warrior and a kind person. Will she not go to Upsala with Ragnhild?"

"She doesn't know. She gave an oath to serve Odin All-Father."

"Think on it, Einar. We can find you land, or we can sail together again. Either way, I will always be your sword, brother. I could never repay what you have done for me."

They drank a cup together, and they needed no more words between them. Hundr tore a leg from a roast chicken at the centre of their table, and its juices ran into his beard as he took a gloriously succulent bite.

Laughter erupted from across the table as Kolo and Brownlegs engaged in an arm wrestle. Kolo was much the bigger man, and Brownlegs' face was as red as a summer apple as he strained to get Kolo's arm down onto the table. Kolo used his free hand to pick food from his plate whilst

Brownlegs strained, and the rest of the crew howled with laughter. Eventually, Kolo slammed Brownlegs' arm down onto the table. He fell in a clatter of wooden plates and cups but then rose, seeming none too worse for wear, and the two men embraced and laughed together.

"I doubt there is a man alive who could best you at that," said Hundr.

"Bjorn," said Kolo, and Hundr nodded in agreement.

"The men like you, Kolo."

"I like them back. You have a good crew, Jarl Rune," Kolo said, and winked at him. Hundr felt a flicker of panic. If Kolo knew he wasn't really the Jarl he claimed to be, he would surely tell Haesten and Erik. He was Haesten's slave, after all.

"Why did you say it like that?"

"Like what?"

"Jarl Rune," Hundr said, mimicking Kolo's voice.

"I am not a fool, my friend. I know your name is Hundr, and that even that isn't your real name. You have another name, an Eastern name that nobody knows. They all take bets on what your name is. Brownlegs here has a silver arm ring on it that says your real name is Karli Sheepshagger," Kolo said, and belly laughed.

"Did you tell Haesten or Erik?"

"No. Haesten wouldn't care once you aren't trying to kill him or take his silver. Erik would kill you for lying, but he wants to kill you, anyway."

"He does?"

"Of course he does. He lives in his brother's shadow, and then you turn up stealing all the glory. He wants to kill you and piss on your bones," Kolo laughed again, "but I won't let him, my friend. So do not worry."

They laughed together again. Hundr relieved that although his secret was out, that it didn't seem to matter too much.

"I want to ask Haesten if he would sell you."

Kolo grinned at him. "To who?"

"To me, of course, you oaf."

"I spoke to Haesten today and asked him for my freedom. I live like a freeman anyway."

"And?"

"He says I can do as I wish, that I am free."

"Did you have to give him silver?"

"No, he says he has enough silver and that I have served him well."

Haesten was a man of surprises. It was rare for such a grim warlord to show kindness to a slave. Hundr smiled broadly and winced as it tugged at his scarring, "You should come with us then, Kolo, join our crew."

159

"I would like nothing more," said Kolo, and they clasped an arm around one another's shoulders and laughed together. Hundr stood and raised his cup again.

"Not another bloody toast," said Blink, shaking his head.

"Sit down. Your voice makes my arse ache," shouted Ragnhild. The entire table laughed. Hundr waited for them to finish and then raised his cup again.

"Kolo is a free man now, and he will join our crew," the table broke into cheers and clapping, "So let's welcome him tonight and drink to our success in Frankia."

They drank and ate until men fell asleep under tables, and the hall became quiet. Haesten made it known that the next day they would march for their ships and that the war for Salomon was over.

The following day was one of sore heads and gathering of treasure. Salomon, Haesten, and Bjorn said their farewells and the Viking army marched out of Le Mans in a long line of warriors shining with silver and gold. They took wagons from the city's merchants just to carry the treasure the army had taken in Frankia. The army marched across Frankia and Brittany, and they were days filled with marching, singing, eating, and drinking. Hundr could not recall a time when he had felt more content. He had the problem of his future to think of, but he had decided it was a good problem. East or not, he had two ships and good friends, and that was enough for now.

The army marched through a wide swathe of farmland and out onto a wide valley, and in the distance, a broad river twinkled in the sun. The men cheered and whooped for joy, for on that river the Viking fleet waited, moored and protected by a handful of crews.

The army paused at the hill's edge, just before a downward slope opened into a verdant valley and down the river itself. There was a commotion at the head of the column, and Hundr quickened his pace to see what it was about. Einar and Kolo followed him, and they pushed and jostled through the throng of men who had paused before descending the slope. Hundr pushed his way between two warriors, and his jaw dropped to his chest.

At a wide point in the river, a host of ships were tied together, looking like a sprawling wooden-water city, filling the river beyond sight and around a meandering bend. But between Haesten and Bjorn's army and their ships waited a Frankish army, an army twice as large as the force they had fought uphill and defeated with ease. Hundr's breath caught in his chest, and all the clamour and noise of the surrounding men vanished as his senses focused on what lay before him. For at the head of that army, Robert the Strong sat aside his grey mount, and next to him was Ivar the Boneless and Sten Slegyya. Ivar was unmistakable with his green cape flapping in the wind and Sten's monstrous frame dwarfed his horse. It had all seemed so simple. The silver almost grew on trees it had been so easy to accumulate. The happiness drained from Hundr, and his dead eye pulsed. For Ivar had come to Frankia, and he was aligned with Duke Robert the Strong, which meant death had come for Hundr and the Seaworm crew.

FOURTEEN

Haesten's forces stood still and were stunned at the appearance of Robert the Strong at the head of a vast army. That enemy force, including Viking warriors under Ivar the Boneless, stood between Haesten, Bjorn, and their precious ships. The shock caused the men to gather in groups, and the sound of their skittish shouting and nervous chatter hummed across the valley.

"Ivar," growled Einar, "I knew the bastard was up to something."

"This is the brother of Bjorn, no?" said Kolo.

"It's his brother," Hundr replied. He couldn't take his eyes off Sten, the old warrior who had been his friend and now rode with his enemy.

"Sten's there too," growled Einar.

"I can see that," Hundr spoke more sharply than he intended.

"This man is the one who was your friend?" asked Kolo.

"He was more like a father than a friend. He came to my aid, with Einar and Ragnhild, when Ivar's son held me captive and took my eye. They stormed a fortress to free me, but then Sten betrayed me to Ivar and took my woman away." As he said those words, he remembered Ivar scoffing when Hundr had referred to Saoirse as "his woman." She was a Princess of Ireland, and she had spoken often of her duty to her people, and at the end, that duty had put a sword into their love, and she had gone with Ivar. What made that heart-rending situation even worse was that Sten had arranged it all.

"He did what he had to do. We are alive because of what he did," said Einar.

"He betrayed me, betrayed us. They both did." Hundr shouted those words at Einar, who held up a hand to show he understood Hundr's point of view.

"I can feel Ivar's blade inside me," Einar said, "I knew he would come."

"I bested him once, and I'll do it again. I hope we fight the bastards. I want to dance in his blood, cut them both to pieces, and piss down their dead throats." Hundr was panting, and he gripped Soulstealer's hilt at his waist.

"Calm, my friend. They go to negotiate, go with

them," said Kolo.

Haesten, Erik, Bjorn, and the two Jarls, Arne and Knut, rode gently down the hillside towards the enemy. Kolo was right. Hundr's place in the army was as a Jarl and he had earned that place through hard fighting, even if his Jarldom was a lie.

"Get me a horse," he said. Kolo sped off and returned quickly astride a black gelding. He jumped from the saddle, and Hundr climbed on. "Who did you take him from?"

"Don't ask," said Kolo, grinning.

Hundr set off to join the leaders, those stony-faced men who went to talk their way out of a fight. Hundr knew that the moment Ivar saw him, there would be no way out, but he wanted that fight. He was a drengr and was sick and tired of running from Ivar and wondering when he would appear to strike the death blow. Better to have the fight now and get it over with. Hundr had Haesten's army behind him, and they had beaten the Franks before. They had been no match for the Viking shield wall that day, and Hundr had no reason to believe today would be any different.

The leaders rode in silence. Even Bjorn's face was stern, with all of his usual good humour vanished. Hundr fell in alongside Erik on the left side of their line, and Haesten's brother shot him a scowl. Hundr ignored him and watched Ivar. Where Robert was calm, patting his grey horse's neck and stroking her ears, Ivar fidgeted in the saddle, and his horse pawed the ground. Ivar's mare became skittish as Hundr and the line of leaders came close, and Ivar sawed at the reins to keep her under control.

"Brother," shouted Bjorn, "you are not keeping good company of late. My ships are behind you."

"I could say the same for you," Ivar replied, and pointed at Hundr. "This bastard is a nithing, and he is mine. Give him up, Bjorn."

"Ivar, I have your sword. I took it from you when I defeated you in single combat. I can beat you again, now if you like," Hundr said. He patted the hilt of Ivar's sword Munin, where it sat strapped to his back.

Ivar's face turned puce, and he urged his horse forward, but Sten held him back.

"I see you are still his nursemaid, Sten the Betrayer. I can fight you too, old man, once I have beaten Ivar."

"Enough," growled Haesten. Then he spoke the Frankish tongue to Robert the Strong, and although Hundr did not understand the words, the gist of it didn't seem too dissimilar to the exchange between him and Ivar. As they spoke together, those two great Lords of War, Hundr ground his teeth and stared at Sten. Sten's head was shaved, save for a long grey plait of hair running from the top of his skull and down his back. Dark dragon tattoos writhed around his ears on the sides of his head and down onto his heavily muscled, bare arms. He wore a coat of mail and held his huge double-bladed axe, Warbringer, at his side. Hundr hated Sten. He hated him because he had been behind the plan that tore Saoirse away, she who he had loved with all his heart and was now wed to Ivar and sat waiting for him in some distant fortress.

"We fight," said Haesten simply, and he wheeled his horse around. Ivar glared at Hundr and spat in his direction. Hundr smiled.

"I'll look for you on the field. Remember though, I beat you, Ivar, so surely I am now the Champion of the North," he said. Ivar went to draw his blade, and Hundr turned away, laughing to follow Haesten and the others. Knowing that he won the verbal exchange with Ivar gave him some comfort, but the thought of Ivar's odd-coloured eyes bearing down on him with blade in hand quenched the laughter, and Hundr felt a squirming in his guts.

"What is it between you and my brother?" asked Bjorn Ironside, falling in beside Hundr.

"We fought together, against the Saxons. We fought back to back at the siege of Jorvik, and Ivar gave me two arm rings for my bravery."

"He hates you, and his hate is not a thing to take lightly."

"We fought against each other at the end. You should know, Lord Bjorn, and it's better to hear it from me than someone else. I killed Ivar's son, Hakon, in single combat. Then I fought Ivar and defeated him, and his men dragged him away. The sword on my back is his, taken from him on that day when he fell to my blade."

Bjorn twisted in the saddle and fixed Hundr with deep brown eyes, searching for the truth. Bjorn chewed at his beard, his mind turning over beneath his broad open face.

"You killed my nephew, and my brother hates you. I should hate you, but I don't. So we'll fight together today and see who's alive at the end." Bjorn nodded at Hundr with clenched teeth, and Hundr nodded his thanks.

"Will you fight your brother?"

"I hope not. I will avoid him if I can. He is my brother."

As the group reached their own lines, Haesten turned his horse, so he faced Hundr, Bjorn, Arne, and Knut. The Jarl leant over his saddle and stroked his horse's neck.

"Robert gave up his towns and cities whilst he waited for the right place to strike," Haesten said. He was calm and seemed unruffled by the prospect of fighting an army that outnumbered his own force by at least two to one. "Robert knows we have to fight. He says he will burn our ships if we flee the field."

"Bastard Frank," growled Bjorn.

"He wants the war over with today. He has your famous brother with him, Bjorn, but Ivar only has two crews. The Franks have fallen to our shield wall before, and I doubt they can stand and trade blows with us this time and win either," Haesten passed a hand through his short, brush-like hair and scratched at his chin, "Robert has chosen the field, and so he has the advantage. He likely has some plan in place to slaughter us, and they have enough men to envelop our flanks if we let them. If they do that, if they win, then we will all die here today."

"We can wait for them here, make them attack up the hill like we did the last time," said Jarl Knut.

"We don't have enough food or water for over one day. They have the river. They can wait us out if they choose." Haesten shook his head. "Jarl Knut, you and one of your crew will take the carts of silver. Robert can't see what we do behind this hill, so take the silver and go around in a wide loop to the North away from the battle. If we win, I will send riders for you."

"If we lose?" asked Knut.

"Then you have your head and are the richest Viking who ever lived," Haesten replied, and others gave a grim chuckle.

"So we fight. We have the hill this time," Bjorn said, staring at where his brother rode to his crews and where the raven banner stood proudly atop a high pole.

"We do," said Haesten, "but we need more than just a head-on attack plan if we are going to win today."

"They picked the ground. There isn't much we can do," said Erik. Which Hundr thought was true. If they had reached the battleground first, they could have dug surprise trenches or hidden riders behind trees or hills.

"All we have to use against them is their hatred," said Haesten. "Robert hates us for his defeat and for ravaging his land. Ivar clearly hates you," he looked at Hundr, "so their hatred will draw them on, and we have the hill. There might also be a chance for a trick or two. Arne, you gather all the horses we have together and ride along the valley bed behind us. Go north and come around in a wide sweep and back along the river's edge. Maybe you can attack them from the flank or rear as they attack us uphill."

Arne nodded and set off to organise his mounted unit.

"The rest of us will make the shield wall and put

our trust in Odin. Ivar's men will have the best chance of breaking our shield wall, and we can't have that happen in the centre of our line, so Rune, you will take the left flank. I will take the middle, and Bjorn, you will take the right. Rune, you must hold Ivar to give us a chance. Bjorn, if you can get through their front rank, then get around their flank and roll them up."

The plan was simple and clear, and Hundr nodded his understanding to Haesten. The Jarl was a clever man, complex and surprising, a different warrior than the usual blunt, brutal Viking leaders. Hundr thought Haesten would make a terrible enemy, and he looked down the hill at his own enemies as they marshalled their ranks for the attack. He felt the twisting heat rising from his belly, the fear. Blades were coming, and blood was coming, and worse of all, Ivar was coming.

Hundr took up his place on the left flank of the army, and he stood in the front rank with Ragnhild on one side and Kolo on the other. Hildr and Hrist were behind them, where they would use their powerful recurved horn bows to rain arrows down on the approaching enemy. Einar took up his place further along the front line with Bush and Blink, with Brownlegs behind them, bow in hand, and shield ready to form the wall. He turned and nodded at Ragnhild, and she nodded back, axe in hand and shield secure on her left arm.

"We will have the gods attention today," she said, and touched the spear amulet for Odin, which hung at her neck. "Few fight against many, Odin will watch, looking for warriors worthy of Valhalla."

"Let's hope he grants us favour," said Hundr, and she rewarded him with a smile. Ragnhild was a fierce and deadly warrior, and he was glad to have her at his side.

"Ivar will try to kill you today," said Kolo.

"I am trying not to think about that."

"What does his name mean, the Boneless? He looked like he has bones to me, my friend."

Hundr laughed. "He is so lithe and quick in battle; blades do not touch him. He moves with speed as though he has no bones and can dance between spears, swords, and axes."

"It is a good name. Look, they are coming."

A horn blared from behind the massed lines of Franks, a strange high-pitched whine to which the Franks let out a roar, and they surged forwards. A drum beat loudly over the massed ranks, and they timed their march to its beat, singing a song of war in their foreign tongue. The effect sent a shudder through Hundr's bones. They looked more formidable than they had in the earlier battle on the hill. Warlord's banners hung at different points through the ranks, and

Hundr assumed Robert had brought those War-lords from across Frankia to bring death to the Vikings.

"Archers, fire at will," Haesten bellowed from down the battle line. The order was shouted again and passed along the line to be heard above the din of the Franks. Ragnhild dropped her shield and put her axe in its belt loop. She took her recurved bow from her back and plucked an arrow from the quiver at her waist.

"Aim for the standards," she said over her shoulder, and Hildr and Hrist both loosed their shafts at the same time. Arrows flew from along the Viking lines, the thrum and whistle of those missiles ringing out above the din of Robert the Strong's war drum. Ragnhild let fly, and below a blue standard wavered and fell, and it was now the Viking's turn to cheer.

Bjorn Ironside marched out beyond the lines, and he waved his axe in defiance at the oncoming enemy. The Vikings waved their own weapons, mirroring Bjorn, and Hundr waved Soulstealer above his head. The Franks let loose their own missiles, and four arrows slammed into the turf, ten paces beyond where Bjorn stood. He laughed, dropped his axe, and pissed towards the enemy. The Viking army hooted with laughter, and Kolo clapped Hundr on the shoulder as he laughed.

"Attack, shield wall, shield wall!" came the order

from down the line again. Hundr swallowed, his throat dry and guts churning. This was the battle fear, but Hundr welcomed it. He knew that in moments, that fear would turn to aggression and battle fury, and a drengr, a lover of battle, welcomed that feeling.

Ragnhild loosed her last shaft, slung her bow over her shoulder, and picked up her shield. Hundr hooked his shield over hers, and Kolo did the same to Hundr's. Hundr clenched his teeth, and his dead eye pulsed. He hoped it pulsed because it knew enemies were close. He had the chance now to fight both Ivar and Sten, and if Ragnhild was right and they had caught Odin's attention, then Hundr would kill them both and send them screaming into Valhalla.

"Keep the line. On me," Einar called, and they moved forward. The Vikings each gave a loud grunt with the step of the march. They would attack downhill, and Hundr hoped the downhill momentum would help them crash into the enemy and drive them backwards. Hundr took two more steps, and then movement in the enemy formation caught his eye.

"Ivar sees us. He's moving to our side," said Hrist over Hundr's shoulder. Hundr saw men shuffling and changing positions before him. Ivar was coming, and there were only thirty paces between them now.

The sky above Hundr dimmed as a wall of arrows launched from the Franks and hurtled towards the Viking front. But because the enemy was marching uphill, most of those shots flew over their targets. Thuds and clicks filled Hundr's ears where shafts punched into shield boards or hit helmets and mail. He heard a few scattered cries amongst the lines behind, but the shield wall held firm. Hundr could see bearded faces beyond the shields of Ivar warriors, he could see their teeth showing where they snarled and the bright tips of their spears and axes as they came on, men who wanted to plunge their blades into his chest and tear his heart out. He had faced such men before, and suddenly the calm descended upon him. Hundr took a deep breath, and he laughed. Ragnhild turned and frowned at him. He couldn't help it, it had all been so easy. The silver flowed like ale at a wedding, and the Vikings had a cut swathe of plunder and victory across Frankia. Now death had come for them, and if it was his time to go to Valhalla, then so be it. But Hundr knew he wouldn't make it easy for them. If they wanted his blood, then they must face his blade.

"Kill, Kill, Kill!" he roared, spittle flying from his mouth.

The shield walls came together in an ear-bursting crunch, and Hundr heaved forwards at the warrior opposite him. That man was tall and bald, and he snarled at Hundr from above his shield. Ragnhild smashed her axe into his skull, and with wide eyes, he mewed like a child, and Hundr laughed again. The pressure on his shield fell away, and he shoved forwards. Kolo grunted as a spear scraped across his mail, and Hundr stabbed Soulstealer towards the enemy.

Hundr moved a few quick steps forward, keeping his shield locked with Ragnhild and Kolo. If they were moving forward, then the enemy was being pushed back, and Hundr stabbed with his sword and pushed with his shield. It was impossible to see beyond the crush of wood on wood. Men shouted, grunted, and died. Hundr could smell sweat and piss, and somewhere over his shoulder a man screamed where a spear cut into his flesh.

A blade beat on Hundr's shield, and he glimpsed a familiar red-bearded face behind it. One of Ivar's Irish warriors from his lands there, the famously vicious Irish fighters were the core of Ivar's crews. Hundr felt a board crack, and he tilted the shield upwards and knelt to slash Soulstealer across Red Beards knees. He howled, and Hundr roared, shoving the falling man out of his way. Hundr surged into the gap and let his shield go. With his free hand, he clawed at an enemy's face and dragged his sword blade across another man's scalp, blood sheeting from the wound covering the man's face in a blanket of thick red liquid. Then there was space around him, and Hundr drew Munin from his back. He parried a spear thrust and slammed his sword into a stocky warrior's belly, and twisted the blade, so it didn't get stuck in his guts. Men suddenly stepped away from him, pushing each other to create a space, and a green cloak caught his eye. A slim warrior with a handsome face stood before him grinning, a man with one blue and one brown eye. Ivar the Boneless.

FIFTEEN

Hundr raised his blades just in time. Ivar held two swords himself, just as he had at the siege of Jorvik, and they came for Hundr fast and flicking like a beast's claws. Hundr parried two blows at the same time and ducked to avoid a back cut, feeling the wind from the sword blade as it passed over his head. He raised Munin to block a thrust at his stomach and leapt back, away from another lunge at his neck. He was sweating and panting hard, and Ivar lowered his swords. The warriors around had stopped fighting to watch the encounter, Hundr risked a glance behind him, and Kolo and Ragnhild stood poised to strike but watching, waiting to see if Hundr could kill Ivar and change the battle.

"Saoirse keeps my bed warm. She is the best woman I've ever had. She moans like a whore when I mount her."

Hundr didn't let him finish. Ivar's words caught

fire in Hundr's chest and burned like Hakon's knife when it took his eye. Ivar was fast, but Hundr knew he was too and let the rage flow through his body. *My turn.* He launched himself at Ivar, whirling his blades and striking out at Ivar high and low, cut and lunge. Ivar parried some blows and dodged away from others, then he came on again, and they traded blows like two dancers flowing around one another in a dance of death.

"Hundr, the line is folding," he heard Ragnhild shout behind him, but he couldn't risk a look. If the line was breaking, he would be caught amongst Ivar's men. He had been so focused on fighting Ivar that Hundr had not realised Ivar's warriors surrounded him. Hundr shuffled backwards and felt a push on his back. They had blocked him in. Ivar came on again, but before the Boneless came within striking distance, Hundr spun and head-butted the warrior behind him and threw that man over his hip and onto Ivar's blade. Hundr spun on his heel, and as he turned, he held his swords outstretched so that each cut across the face of a warrior on either side of him. He heard one man scream, and one blade clanked on a helmeted face. Hundr kept on moving and leapt towards his own line. He could see Kolo and Ragnhild cutting at the enemy, trying desperately to reach him.

Hundr had left chaos behind him, and he

watched Ivar shouting, red-faced and incoherent trying to get through his own men to strike at Hundr, but then Ragnhild hefted her shield in front of him, closely followed by Kolo, and suddenly Hundr was back behind his own shield wall.

"We have to retreat. The line has buckled. Sten is there," Ragnhild said, her face twisted into a grimace and splashed with blood.

"Back then, keep order, one step at a time," Hundr said. So they shuffled backwards and disengaged from the enemy. Hundr looked over Kolo's shoulder, and there he was, Sten. The old man swung his monstrous double-bladed war axe and beat it upon Bush and Blink's shield, his monstrously wide shoulders rising and falling like boulders in a landslide.

"Where's Einar? Fall back," Hundr said. He couldn't see Einar, and beyond where Bush tried to keep Sten at bay, Hundr could see the sheer volume of Franks was driving the Viking shield wall back up the hill. He couldn't see Bjorn or Haesten, just a mass of shields and blades and blood-soaked warriors.

"Retreat, but don't turn your backs," he said, and so they did.

Ivar's warriors broke off the assault, and the lull in fighting allowed them to take a breath. So Hundr and the Seaworm crew could back off ten paces, then twenty paces. Then they were at the top of the hill, and all Hundr could see was carnage. Bodies littered the hill, some dead and still, but most writhing and screaming amongst the pools of piss and blood. They had churned the once green hillside into a slick, brown mess, and beyond the horror of the wounded, Robert the Strong and Ivar marshalled their lines to attack once more.

"Knut didn't come, the bastard," said Kolo, spitting a curse.

"He didn't attack?" said Hundr.

"No, he must have taken his riders and gone after the treasure wagons."

Hundr looked down at the enemy. There were still too many. He couldn't tell which side had the best of the fighting, but the Franks had thrown them back, and without Knut attacking the enemy flanks with his mounted warriors, Hundr could not see a way for the Vikings to win.

"Retreat carefully, hold the line," he said to Ragnhild. "I have to find Haesten and Bjorn." She nodded, and Hundr set off at a run.

He skirted around the rear ranks, where men were turning to run from the horror. He saw some of Guthmund's men amongst them. Hundr ignored the runners. Most men don't like to fight. They do it because they have to, but most prefer to stand at the back and strike only when it's safe to do so. Only the wild men, the lovers of battle, fight at the front where the blades strike and a man earns his reputation, or his place in Valhalla. So, it did not surprise him to see some turn and flee in the face of the sheer number of Franks before them. But if the entire army turned and ran, then the day would turn red with slaughter. The Franks would chase them and cut them down without mercy.

Hundr found Haesten and Bjorn in heated conversation at the centre of the battle line. Bjorn was gesticulating wildly, his axe coated in filth and gore, and he had a deep gash on his forehead.

"Attack them. I am the son of Ragnar Lothbrok, and I do not run. We fight!" Bjorn was shouting, and Haesten raised a hand to calm him.

"We all want to fight and go to Valhalla, Bjorn, but we can live. We can live to fight another day," said Haesten.

Hundr reached them, and Bjorn glared at him, eyes bulging and teeth bared.

"Robert and Ivar just want us," Hundr said. "If we retreat into the valley bed, let most of the army peel off to the South, and we three with a few men will head east. They will follow us, and the army will live." Hundr said. He knew Ivar would follow him, Ivar would chase him to the ends of the earth to slake his thirst for vengeance, and he supposed it was the same for

Robert the Strong in his hatred for Haesten and Bjorn.

"It might work," said Haesten, rubbing his eyes.

"I don't run," Bjorn said, growling through the bush of his beard.

"We aren't running. We retreat and draw off the main army. Our army survives, and if we can elude Robert, then we can fight again. On our terms, on a field of our choosing." Hundr said.

"He's right. Bjorn, you have to listen. If we retreat now, we can fight again and win. If we stand and fight here, then we die, and all we have fought for is lost."

Bjorn looked at Haesten, then at Hundr, and then at the Franks. He pushed his head back and roared at the top of his voice, his body shaking like some mighty bear denied its prey.

"Come on then," said Bjorn.

The army split just as Hundr said they should. He marched in a group with Bjorn and Haesten, along with Kolo, Ragnhild, and a dozen of Bjorn and Haesten's men, handpicked for their fighting skill. Einar kept the rest of the Seaworm crew with the army. Splitting the Viking force confused the Franks and bought the Vikings enough time to put distance between them and the enemy. Hundr's plan gave Robert a puzzle to chew over. It would push him to decide what to do next and then convince Ivar of that decision. He had to decide between splitting his own forces to finish the main Viking force and its leaders separately, or sending his whole army after the leaders, and then what to do about the Viking fleet. Robert would also have to leave enough men at the river in case the Vikings doubled back and simply sailed away. They were not decisions to take lightly, and Hundr hoped that problem, and the time it would take Robert to issue orders and organise his troops, might give the Vikings enough time to slip away.

Hundr and Bjorn made sure Robert and Ivar saw they were present in the smaller group by taunting them from the high ground. As Bjorn, Kolo, and the other warriors waved their weapons in challenge at the Franks, Hundr and Haesten searched the surrounding landscape. From the hilltop, they could see the sweep of the valley leading across the battlefield and down to the ships, then away to the North into thick forest ranging as far as Hundr could see, to the south lay open farmland and fields of crops.

"There," said Haesten, pointing back to the East, "That town has a church, a big one."

"We have to keep moving. If we stop, they will surround us in that church, storm it, and butcher us," said Hundr.

"We don't have a choice. If we keep running,

they will bring up horses from their rear and ride us down. We gave all our mounts to Knut."

Haesten was right, they had no horses, so the Franks would have them chased down before afternoon turned to evening. Knut had taken all the horses the Vikings possessed but had not brought that force of cavalry around to attack the Franks from the flanks. He had fled to save his own skin.

"He might have gone after the treasure carts."

"Can't think about that now. If we get to that church, we can at least make it hard for them to get in and kill us. It's a stone building, and their numbers won't matter if they try to storm the doors and windows. You can't see it from here, but I remember it from the march inland."

"Surely they will just burn the thatch with us inside?"

"They won't burn a church. They love their Christ God too much, so we will need to keep some of those dress-wearing Priests in there with us."

"Maybe, if we can survive today, we can get out, and get away," said Hundr, which was as much as they could hope for. The Franks' choices were limited. They either stormed the church, burned it, or starved them out. And maybe, a slim maybe, the Vikings could sneak away.

"It's our only chance," said Haesten.

The Viking leaders marched towards the small town at double time. They moved as fast as was possible under the weight of their arms and armour. Leaving shields or mail behind would mean death if it came to a fight again with the pursuing Franks. Hundr thought, as did the others, that even if the Franks rode them down in large numbers, as long as they had their weapons, they could put up a fight. They could die with their blades in their hands and wake up in Odin's Hall, together again where they would feast and fight together until the end of days.

Hundr kept time with Ragnhild and Kolo. They took four normal marching steps and then four quick steps. The small force marched in grim silence. All Hundr could hear was the rattle and clank of weapons and the laboured breathing of warriors as they made for the town. He could see it now, nothing more than a wide scrape of muddy laneway flanked on either side by buildings, blacksmith's, bakers, and merchants, and then at the end of that line of buildings, there was a stone church, just as Haesten said there would be.

The group reached the town, and the Church itself reared up before them. It was a dull, grey stone building, twice as tall as a man with a high gabled front. An enormous cross sat at the apex, and greying thatch covered the roof. It didn't look like much, but it was their only hope.

"They're coming," a warrior shouted from the rear.

Hundr looked over his shoulder, and sure enough, he saw riders pounding through a field of wheat.

"Pick up the pace, run if you can," said Haesten.

Hundr ran. There was no shame in it, or at least he told himself so. A drengr does not run, but surely it was better to run and live, to strike at your enemies again, than stand to die like a fool. The pursuing horses pounded the ground, the sound rumbling like thunder and getting louder at every heartbeat. They were close to the Church, and Hundr could see tall doors made of golden, polished oak. He was so close he could make out the black rivets on the door hinges, so he ran. He ran and burst through the doors.

The timber doors swung open with a groan which echoed around the stone walls. Inside were two lines of dark wooden benches, and at the top of those rows were the altar and another gigantic cross. A gaggle of Priests knelt at the benches, and they spun as Hundr burst through the doors, their mouths falling open, hands clasped together before their chests as they prayed to their God.

"Grab four of them," Hundr snarled, and he and Kolo raced forward. The Priests shouted and tried to scatter, but Kolo threw his shield at them, and two fell. As two more bent to help their friends, Kolo took them prisoner, allowing the others to scuttle away through a small door behind the altar. The rest of the Viking force charged into the building, panting and shouting, and Bjorn pushed the doors closed whilst two of his men dragged benches over to barricade the entrance.

"They'll try to charge us," said Bjorn, red-faced and sweating from the frantic dash to the Church.

"There, the windows. Bring more benches," said Ragnhild. She had taken as many arrows as she could collect before the army split into two, and she had spare quivers slung over both shoulders. Some of Haesten's men also carried bows, and so they dragged benches to the high shuttered windows which faced onto the enemy approach. Ragnhild jumped up on a bench, flung open the shutters, and in one fluid movement she un-slung her bow, nocked an arrow, and fired at the Franks.

"Good," said Haesten, nodding in appreciation at Ragnhild's quick work. "Now, they will need to be cautious."

"They will still try, behind a shield wall," said Hundr.

"They will, but we can hold them."

They held them. The day stretched, and the Franks came on, but a hail of arrows from Ragnhild and Haesten's men repulsed them. The Franks made it to the doors on three occasions, but the Vikings braced those doors with benches and their own strength, and so the Church held fast. Then Bjorn brought a Priest to one window, and Haesten shouted in the tongue of the Franks that they would kill the Priests if the Franks attacked again, and the onslaught halted.

Hundr watched as more and more of the enemy gathered in the town and surrounded the Church. He saw the large shields, with their Raven painted white over leather shield covers, and he knew Ivar had come. The plan had worked, and surely most of the Viking army escaped the slaughter. But he was trapped now, holed up in a church and surrounded by hundreds of enemy warriors.

Darkness fell, and Bjorn made a small fire in the centre of the church floor. He chopped up a bench with his axe and used flint and steel to get a blaze going. The light and warmth were welcome as the dark drew in. Hundr slumped his back against the cold stone wall. His shoulders ached from fighting, and his dead eye throbbed pain deep into his skull. They were seventeen warriors, trapped like rats in what must surely become a stone tomb. When morning came, Ivar and Robert would start the assault proper, they would throw all their warriors at the Church, and seventeen must hold against hundreds. How long could they hold before they were overwhelmed? He closed his good eye and imagined himself captured and falling under Ivar's knife. He remembered the Northumbrian King Aelle and how Ivar had cut the blood eagle on the King's back. The King lifted on ropes, so all could see where Ivar had opened his back with a sharp knife and carefully chiselled away the king's ribs, one at a time whilst Aelle still lived. Ivar had peeled the skin away and opened Aelle's rib cage out, so his back splayed wide like an eagle's wings. No doubt Ivar had some such ingenious torture planned for Hundr. *I will die first. I will die with my sword in my hand and take as many bastards with me as I can.*

SIXTEEN

The onset of darkness brought a long bloody day of combat to an end. Hundr knelt on the chill stone floor and used a strip of cloth, torn from a Priest's robe, to bind a gash on Ragnhild's thigh. Most of the warriors locked up in the church bore wounds from the furious onslaught the Franks launched against its walls. Bjorn Ironside had lost the tip of a finger. Kolo's shoulder was torn open where a spear blade had found its mark. Hundr bound Ragnhild's thigh tight, and she grunted her thanks as he finished the knot.

"More than a few arrows came through the windows. I'll see what I can find," she said.

"Can you walk on it?" he asked as she tested her weight on the leg.

"I have two legs. A drengr doesn't limp," she said. She took a few halting steps, clenched her teeth, and strode off to find any spent enemy arrows. Ragnhild had used up all the quivers she had carried into the church. Hundr shook his head. He had never felt so weary, and Ragnhild seemed ready to fight again despite her wound. Hundr had come away unscathed, save for a few scratches and bruises.

"We need to take watches through the night," said Haesten, pacing the length of the church, "one man on watch at north, southeast, and west. They might come at us deep in the darkness when weariness overcomes us and sleep tries to dull our wits."

"They are everywhere, all around," said Bjorn. "I see my brother and his men out there. They will burn the thatch soon. Burn us out."

"They won't. The Franks won't let them burn the church," said Haesten. Hundr agreed they wouldn't burn their holy ground. Not with the Priests held hostage inside. Haesten busied himself organising the turns for watch duty, and he had his men make a collection of any food, ale, and water the warriors had carried into the church or whatever they could find within the building.

Hundr walked to the centre of the church and sat next to Kolo, who was keeping the small fire going with strips of wood chopped from the church benches. The big man smiled at him.

"That was a rare fight, my friend."

"It was. We are lucky to have only lost two men,"

said Hundr. Two of Bjorn's men had fallen at the south window, where Ivar's warriors, including Sten, had almost forced their way in. Sten himself had killed one of Bjorn's men with a spear thrust to the throat. The old warrior had one hand inside the window and was about to hurl himself through the space before Bjorn shoved him back with his shield. Another of Bjorn's men had fallen at that same window with an arrow in his eye. That left fifteen of them trapped inside.

"They'll come again," said Kolo.

"We need to think of a way out, and it has to be tonight. We can't hold another day. Cover of night is our best bet."

"You have seen the flames outside. They have us surrounded with fire."

Kolo was right, and Hundr could see the flickers of those fires dancing against the dark timbers of the church's roof where the fire's glare came in through the window holes. The Franks had set up a perimeter of high fires all around the church, so that even as the shroud of darkness fell across the land, the church was still lit and visible. Hundr had taken a peek out of a western window before he tended to Ragnhild, and he could see the grim, bearded faces staring on from behind the firelight. The Franks had lost men in their attacks on the church. Robert the Strong paced the perimeter in his fine bronze fish scale armour urging his warriors on to the attack, and they had thrown themselves at the church's openings. Ragnhild and the other Viking archers had made each arrow count, and more than one Frank peeled away from the attack with a shaft buried in thigh, neck, or shoulder. The fighting at the windows had been a shoving match of blades and shields. No skill was needed for that. They had all taken a turn at the windows, and every one of them had fought and pushed and kept the enemy at bay.

"We might get our chance in the deep of the night."

Ragnhild came to join them. "Twenty good arrows, we'll need to make them count," she said, shaking her quiver full of Frankish shafts scavenged from the church floor. She slid down to sit next to Kolo, keeping her wounded leg straight.

"Women do not fight where I come from," said Kolo. Ragnhild rewarded him with a frown above her one-eyed face.

"Well, they do where I come from."

"Your face is pretty when you are angry," said Kolo, and Hundr coughed with surprise. Ragnhild was a lot of things, but with the crisscross scarring across her face combined with her missing eye, pretty was not one of them. She shifted uncomfortably and pointed a finger at Kolo.

"If you value your head, you won't talk like that

to me again."

"I apologise. I cannot help it. I like you, Ragn-hild. You are fierce and proud like a lion."

"What's a lion?" she said, and Kolo laughed, his deep booming voice bouncing off the church walls.

"It is an animal from my homeland, the king of the beasts with sharp teeth and claws and a roar to shake the mountains."

She seemed to soften to that comparison. "Is it much like here, your home?"

"No, not like here. We don't have swords, or ships, or armour. We live simpler, but our war-riors are just as brave. My people don't crave treasure and land like you pale skins do. You are driven mad with greed."

"Haesten must have sailed far to get to your home?" Ragnhild asked.

"He sailed far south, yes, but not to my home. My home is very far south, my friends. A week's march beyond the great sea. Other men captured me, and Haesten bought me as a slave on the coast. Now I am here, with you blood-mad Vi-kings." Kolo said and smiled.

Haesten, Bjorn, and the warriors not on first watch gathered around the fire, and what lit-tle food they had was shared out. There were hard oatcakes and some dried meat and sausage.

There was a half-full wineskin and another skin of water.

"It will be a long night, with more fighting at daybreak," growled Bjorn. All his good humour had ebbed away in the retreat from Robert's army.

"We are in a grim spot for sure," said one of Haesten's men, Rollo, a short warrior with thinning blonde hair and a long stringy beard.

"We've been in worse," said another.

"We all remember the storm, the fury of Njorth," said a tall, broad-shouldered Dane. Njorth was the sea god, and Hundr remembered that Haesten and Bjorn had been caught in a great storm in the south, and they had lost half of their fleet of ships. The warriors went quiet at the stirring of that memory.

"Nothing could be as bad as that," said Bjorn, lost in a daze, staring into the flames. "Drifting for days at the gods' mercy, tossed around the Whale Road like a child's wooden toy. Nothing to see but rain and white-tipped waves. Nothing to hear but the roar of the sea, the cracking and snapping of ships, and the screaming of our brothers."

"Nothing can be as bad as that," agreed Rollo. "At least here we can die with our blades, where the gods can see us." The rest of the warriors nodded.

"Enough talk of those days," said Haesten, standing before the fire, his wide slash of a mouth turned down at the corners and his eyes bright. "We have to get out of this place, or die trying."

"I say we charge out at first light," said Bjorn, "hold the cursed Christ Priests in front of us. Drive at the Franks, not at my brother's men. Break through and fight our way free of this shithole."

The gathered warriors grumbled their approval at Bjorn's plan.

"One or two warriors could get away when the night is well along. Get away and find the army. Maybe there will be time to march them back here," said Haesten.

"One, maybe two could make it," Hundr said. They had to try. The army couldn't be too far away. Whoever left the church, if they made it through the lines of Franks guarding the church, would simply follow the track they had taken back to the battlefield and pick up the army's trail. So many men marching would leave a stain on the countryside, the fields would be churned to mud underfoot, and marching men always left detritus on the road, empty skins of ale, broken boots, and other discarded items.

"They can't be more than a half day's march away," said Haesten.

"So the army could be here by nightfall tomorrow," said Bjorn, "then we break out of his cursed place and let these bastards feel our steel."

"I will go," Ragnhild said. Haesten looked at the Valkyrie, his bright eyes fixed on her, the possibilities and eventualities of sending her on this crucial mission turning over in his sharp mind. Then he nodded his assent. If anyone could slip out of the church, get through the enemy lines by stealth or by blade, it was Ragnhild.

"I will go with you," Kolo said. Ragnhild opened her mouth as though to protest, but she stopped herself. Kolo was a huge and formidable warrior, and she would need his fighting skills if the Franks cornered them.

"So we have to survive one more day in this place," said Rollo.

"They will throw everything at us, try to swarm us. They might even convince themselves to burn the thatch," said Haesten.

"Then we need to remind them they will burn their holy men alive," said Bjorn, "We should tie them into the thatch, where they can be seen, and their screams heard by all. Then these pious bloody fools will think twice about burning us alive if they have to watch and hear their Priests burn."

Hundr looked at the four Priests, huddled and shaking in a dank corner of the church. Bjorn was right. They had to use the hostages to buy them time, and putting them on show somewhere on the thatched roof would discourage Robert and his men from throwing flaming torches up there. Ivar would have no such worries, but men who worshipped the Christ God held their Priests in reverence and could not let them burn. The thought of Ivar made him shiver. That vision of the blood eagle was etched on Hundr's eyelids. He remembered Ivar's odd eyes during the battle, how he had fought with controlled fury.

"I can't let him take me," he whispered.

"Who?" asked Ragnhild.

"Ivar. When they storm this place tomorrow, I can't let him take me."

She nodded. "You took his reputation, and you killed his son."

"If it comes to it tomorrow, I must make sure I die before falling into his hands." Hundr knew now it had to be that way. If Ragnhild and Kolo could not bring the army back in time to attack the Franks who besieged the church, and if he thought for a second that the Vikings inside the church would be overwhelmed, then he would throw himself upon an enemy blade. He would make sure he did not fall into Ivar's hands alive if nothing else.

"The gods toy with us," Ragnhild said, fixing

Hundr with her eye. "We thought we had it all. We thought we were the Lords of war, fat with silver and glory. Marching through this country as though nothing could touch us. The Norns watched. They sat below the great tree Yggdrasil, which holds up the world. Those three spinners of our fates looked upon our pride and they laughed."

"We are not dead yet, my friends," said Kolo, and he lifted his chin. "All this talk of death and the gods. We are still alive. We are all warriors. I saw you fight with Ivar the Boneless today and you were his equal. We can fight our way out of this. Ragnhild and I will wait until the dark and cold creep across the Franks' skins. Then we will slip away in the dark corners, and when we come back, we will paint our blades red with their blood."

Hundr smiled at his friend. He was right. All was not yet lost. Hundr left Ragnhild and Kolo to make their plan of how they would get out of the church and through the Franks. He went and stood next to Haesten. The Jarl was at the far gable end of the church. Hundr approached and saw that Haesten was flicking through the pages of a thick leather-bound book. They had such things in the east, Hundr had seen them in Novgorod where the Christ priests became ever more present in the city. They were tolerated because they paid huge tithes and because there were many Christian slaves in the city, and allowing their religion kept the slaves content. Haesten thumbed through the pages, brushing his hand over the finely crafted words and beautifully coloured pictures of beasts and men.

"They are clever, these Priests, they write everything down. We write nothing, save the saga's and tales of the gods."

"What would you write, Lord, if you could?"

"We rely on word of mouth, of our men repeating our words and orders as we say them. With this," Haesten said, tracing the words with his fingertips, "a man can be sure that his words are carried and preserved exactly as he wants them to be."

Hundr watched Haesten's eyes move over the page. He had not seen Haesten fight in the front line or distinguish himself in battle like Bjorn, or even Ivar would. Haesten was different. His weapon was his mind.

"When did you learn the Franks' language?"

"When I arrived here, as I did in the south with the Muslim men. How can we think like and understand our enemy if we do not speak their language?"

Haesten was a frightening man. Hundr didn't feel physically threatened by Haesten, and he wasn't prone to bouts of rage and violence. But his calmness, his cleverness, was a thing to be feared. It gave Hundr comfort that he fought beside Haesten and not against him. He would make a formidable enemy. *I have enough of those.*

"You are not who you said you were. Why does Ivar hate you?"

"My men call me Hundr, not Jarl Rune. I am not a Jarl. I came to you whilst on the run from Ivar. He cornered my ship close to the coast, and I jumped ship to draw him off and save my crew."

"The other ship?" Haesten said, turning a page gently and not taking his eyes from the book.

"I attacked it, killed its crew. So I knew it would be there in the river unless the Franks had found it."

"So, who are you?"

Good question. "I am from the East, from Novgorod, and ran from home to join a Viking crew. I started at the bottom and worked my way up to Carl and then made my reputation in the war against the Saxons."

"Which is where you met Ivar?"

"Which is where I met Ivar. I fought for him, and he rewarded me with two arm rings, which were taken from me by his son. His son took me, took my eye. Ragnhild and my men freed me, and I killed Hakon Ivarsson. I fought Ivar, one against one, and I defeated him. This is his sword,"

Hundr said, reaching up to tap the hilt of Munin across his shoulder, "he is the champion of the Northmen and I beat him."

"You killed his son and stole his reputation. So he hates you."

"He does, and our fates are intertwined now. One of us must kill the other, neither will have peace until that happens."

Haesten nodded and raised his head to meet Hundr's gaze. "I don't care that you are not a Jarl. In this world, a man can be whatever he wants to be. I came from nothing and fought my way to wealth and reputation. I had thirty ships when I left the Muslims, more than most kings can boast. You can be whatever you have it in yourself to be, as long as you can defend that claim. If I say you are a slave and want to put you in irons, it will be so unless you have enough force, enough skill, or enough warriors to deny that claim. So, I don't care that you are not a Jarl. You fight well and have a quick mind. But never take me for a fool, Hundr." The corners of Haesten's wide mouth flicked downwards, and his gaze was firm beneath his white eyebrows raised and knitted below a furrowed forehead. Hundr nodded his agreement. He wanted to ask Haesten where he came from and where he had started his journey to wealth and power, but he saw in the firm set of Haesten's jaw that he would talk no more of such things.

"I won't let Ivar take me alive."

"I won't let Robert take me alive. There will be a moment, either this night or during tomorrow's fighting. There will be a moment for us to break out. We must be ready to seize that chance. It might be your friend and Kolo can bring our men back to attack the Franks. It might be the enemy leave a space between watches, or a man falls asleep at his post. We must search for that moment and be decisive. I have my men on alert, and they know what to look for. Keep yourself alert, Hundr. Be ready."

Hundr would be ready, and he hoped Haesten was right. He doubted they could get through the entire day tomorrow against such overwhelming numbers. But he had made peace now with the hard truth of his situation. They must break out and escape or die on Frankish blades. There could be no surrender, no capture. It was escape or death.

SEVENTEEN

Ragnhild and Kolo slipped away in that ethereal time between deep night and dawn when the Sun hasn't yet shown itself, but its glow casts a pale red and gold hue across the horizon. The Franks had not attacked during the night, so confident were they that they trapped the Viking leaders inside the church. Their fires burned bright at first, in a tight ring around the church's perimeter, but as the night drew on and the third watch came around, those fires dwindled in brightness. Warriors on watch added less fuel to the fires, because it meant cutting more wood, and they could see the Franks warming their hands against the night chill and cuffing at tired eyes.

Hundr helped drop Ragnhild and Kolo from a small, west-facing window. He and Rollo lowered them slowly, one at a time, so there was no thud onto the grass, no jangling of weapons. They picked that window because the fire opposite had waned to nothing more than a shin-high campfire. Its dancing brightness barely reached the stone walls, and Ragnhild believed that was the best point to try for. So, Hundr helped them down and then watched as she and Kolo crawled slowly on their bellies, keeping flat on the dirt. Ragnhild was cautious, and she made her way slowly, like an old beetle edging slowly across the grass. She would shuffle forwards, then pause for twenty heartbeats and wait for a sound, and then go again. Once she and Kolo had passed out of sight, Hundr sat against the wall and listened. *Odin, let them make it. Hear me, All-Father.* Hundr closed his eyes, and Odin surely heard his prayer, because the alarm never went up. Hundr sat and gripped tight to Soulstealer's hilt in its scabbard. He listened, and he waited, but there were no shouts, no screams, no clashes of arms.

"Sounds like they made it," said Rollo, grinning.

"I wouldn't have chosen any other than Ragnhild for the job. It would take ten of them to stop her." That was a boast, and Hundr knew it, but she was the finest and fiercest warrior he had ever seen. Even though she'd taken a wound to her thigh, she would still make it. The church was quiet, deathly quiet. Some of Bjorn and Haesten's men who weren't on watch dozed by the small fire. The priests also dozed, heads leaning on one another. Hundr looked over at Bjorn Ironside. He sat on a bench, with his axe resting on the stone floor, where he spun it around in his palm so it turned quickly, making a barely audible whirring sound. Hundr had met Bjorn's brothers in Northumbria, Ivar, Ubba, and Sigurd Snake Eye. All famous warriors, men of will and reputation.

As he watched Bjorn, Hundr wondered how it must have been for them growing up, those sons of a famous father. They had all grown to be men in their own right, respected and feared. Then he remembered his own childhood, his father's legitimate sons preening and flouncing in silks and soft boots. They had taunted him, bastard that he was. He could hear his old Rus Viking name Velmud echoing across the halls and training grounds of Novgorod. They were no match for the sons of Ragnar. Those sons, and the other noblemen's sons who learned weapon and lore craft alongside him, were cruel to Hundr. They teased his poor clothes and his status. Many nights he had lain in his straw bed, outside the soft warmness of Novgorod's palace, and cursed his father and those other boys. His only joy in those days had been his own skill. He had excelled at weapons training. Above all the other boys, he was the fastest and the fiercest. When he fled his home, slinking out of the city with a pouch of stolen hack silver, he was sure nobody would be sad to see him gone. None would miss Velmud, the Bastard. Hundr had made that long journey across the wilds and villages to get to the coast and find a trading ship who would take him on board. He remembered cold, fear-filled nights on the plains and in the forests, sneaking into a barn or breaking into a farmhouse to steal food. All those memories had brought him here, to Frankia, where Ivar had him cornered.

On the march from Le Mans, Hundr had walked with light steps, certain of his plan to go east, to go home and show his father how important and wealthy he had become with two ships, two swords, and a bilge full of silver. Now he had nothing again, nothing but his swords and his skill. Hundr remembered what Ragnhild had said about the Norns and how they laughed at men and wove their fate. Now that dream of sailing home lay in ruins, a foolish dream smashed by Ivar's boot. As he sat there in the twilight hour, his eyes stinging and heavy from lack of sleep, and his skin dusted with the oily film that comes from a long night without rest, he realised he only had one goal, one ambition to accomplish. He had to kill Ivar the Boneless. As long as Ivar was alive, there could be no peace. Sten, too, was Hundr's enemy, but not like Ivar.

He remembered Sten's face, long and sorrowful when he betrayed Hundr in Northumbria. It was hard to admit, but sitting alone on the cold stone floor, he knew Sten had done what he had thought best to save Hundr, Einar, and

Ragnhild's life. But it didn't make it hurt any less. If Ivar was dead, then Hundr was sure Sten would melt away, retreat to the quiet life Einar's crew had ripped from him. They had found him living peacefully with Christ Monks in the Northumbrian countryside. Einar and his men had killed the monks, but recognising Sten as a hero of old, they had carried him off to join the war against King Aelle. Hundr missed Sten. He missed his surly, curt responses to questions, he missed the old man looking out for him. As he looked around the dark corners of the church's recesses, Hundr missed Sten's company. He was alone now, here with Bjorn, Haesten, and their men. He did not know these warriors. They had sailed together for years and were as close as brothers; together, they had suffered the unspeakable horrors of a great sea storm where half of their brothers were lost to the depths under the howling winds and crashing waves. Hundr had no one close. He had loved Saoirse, and the gods had torn them apart. Sten was lost to him. He was as he had always been, alone in the cold, with only himself to rely on.

Hundr sniffed and rubbed the sting from his eyes. He groaned and stood, touching gently at his scar and dead eye, the skin there as tender as always. He stood on the bench he and Rollo had used to lower Ragnhild and Kolo earlier, and he peered out into the night. Only it was not night anymore. The sun had poked its rim above the distant hills, and the land beyond the church, the hills and fields Hundr had marched across the day before, was washed in a dull and still half-light. He heard bird song somewhere out of sight, but there at the fire in front of his window, just out of bowshot, was Robert the Strong. The big Frankish Lord drank from a steaming cup, two hands held around its rim for warmth, and with him were two other straight-backed men, men with trimmed beards and fine tunics. Robert stood with his lords, the Lords of Frankia, who had heeded his call and brought their warriors to put the infernal Vikings in the ground. Those three lords stood there, without their armour, and spoke softly together, looking at the church and at their siege positions.

This is the chance. This is the one chance Haesten knew would come. Hundr jumped from the bench and strode to Bjorn.

"He's out there, without his mail and unprotected," Hundr said, his voice echoing in the rafters.

"What?" Bjorn stopped spinning his axe and frowned at Hundr.

"Robert the Strong is there. We can get at him."

Bjorn jumped to his feet and ran to the bench. He stepped up and peered out of the window.

"The arrogant bastard," growled Bjorn. He

turned to Hundr, muscles under his beard working where Bjorn set his jaw.

"We can get to him. If we kill him, they are leaderless. That gives us a chance, buys us time."

Hundr wanted it. He wanted to charge out of the church, blade in hand, to strike at his enemies. He hated being stuck in the cold building, with only his thoughts for his company. Much like when he had sailed away from Northumbria with the pain of Saoirse and Sten still cut deep into his heart, he could only find solace in battle, in the cold calmness of battle joy, and he yearned for that now. He was tired of waiting for Ivar, with the threat of capture and torture hanging over his head.

"We could kill him," Bjorn stared at Hundr, and nodded his head slowly. He glanced at his wounded finger and then back to Hundr. "That would at least be a good boast to take to Valhalla. They have another leader, though. My brother is there."

"The Franks won't follow Ivar."

"They won't," conceded Bjorn. "Ivar must hate your bones to go up against me like this. We were never close, but we are still brothers."

Hundr felt his dead eye pulsing, as it did now at any mention of Ivar and his hate. "Do you want to kill Duke Robert or not?" Hundr said, and he drew Soulstealer, her blade scraping on the wooden scabbard, and Hundr felt all the eyes in the church turn to him. "I, for one, am tired of skulking behind these walls like a rat. I am a drengr. I stormed the walls of Jorvik, and I killed Hakon Ivarsson with his own blade, this blade. I fought and bested Ivar the Boneless, Champion of the North, in single combat. I do not hide from Franks." The men stood now, and Haesten took a step toward him. Bjorn nodded and raised his axe. Even though Hundr was his brother's enemy, Bjorn was a drengr and Hundr had called to that deep-seated warrior's pride.

"What is this?" asked Haesten.

"It is that moment, Lord. The one moment you spoke of. Look, see for yourself," said Hundr, and Haesten stepped onto the bench and peered at the Franks.

"He is there. His guard is down. Whoever goes out there might not get back," said Haesten.

"I will go. Open the doors and I will charge at the bastard and cut him down and his fancy Lords in their women's clothes. I am a drengr and I will cut them down and watch them bury their Lord. This I will do, or I will die trying, and then I will wait for you in Valhalla where we will share a horn of ale and laugh about this day." Hundr knew he spoke boastfully, but he spoke to them all and their pride. He wanted the fight, he wanted the reputation of killing Duke Robert, and he did not care if he lived or died. *Who would shed a tear for me when I am gone? Who would care that I am cold and dead in the ground?*

"I will go with you. We will do this thing together, you and I. Let's kill the bastard," said Bjorn.

And so, moments later, Hundr stood at the altar. He had Soulstealer in his right hand, and a shield held firm in his left. Bjorn stood with him, axe and shield poised. They both wore Brynjar mail coats, and they were ready.

"If you can do this, they will be in disarray. It might buy us enough time if Ragnhild and Kolo can fetch the army."

Or we will die.

"Open the doors," shouted Bjorn, and they pulled the oak doors open. Hundr took a deep breath and set off at a run with Bjorn. They ran through the church, through the doors, and out into the wan sunlight, and there before them was Duke Robert the Strong, who turned to see the charge and his cup fell from his fingers.

The Duke saw two brutal men charging at him. Two warriors with swords and axe and shields. Bjorn was a big, bushy-bearded frightening man, and Hundr knew that he too was not fair to look upon with his scar ravaged face and one eye. The Franks just stared as the two blood mad Vikings sprinted from the church and closed the gap too fast, before the Lords or their soldiers with their minds, befuddled by lack of sleep, could react to the threat.

"Keep moving," Hundr said between quick intakes of breath. Bjorn was at his shoulder and was keeping pace, and Hundr spoke to calm his racing heart more than to make sure Ironside kept up.

"Archers!" Bjorn bellowed. Hundr heard the twang of bowstrings from behind, and, as planned, two of Haesten's men shot from the open windows on either side of the church door. They aimed at the warriors who were on watch, and one of those men now fell to his knees with a shaft in his foot.

Ahead, Hundr saw Robert drawing his sword. He was a big man, as large as Bjorn, and his face turned from wide-mouthed surprise to twisted anger. The three Lords stood there in the morning light and seemed slight and thin without their mail. Robert drew his blade, but the two other Lords took a step back. More arrows whistled past Hundr, and they were almost there. There was shouting amongst the Frankish ranks now. They were stirring to action, but they were too late. A Frank charged Hundr with a levelled spear. He roared as he charged and his spear thudded into Hundr's shield, stopping him for a moment. Bjorn swung his axe backhand and the heavy blade chopped through the spearman's face, slicing off his nose and spraying blood across Hundr's shield. Hundr leapt over the falling man, and they were there.

Hundr swung Soulstealer, and Robert parried the blow. The Duke spun to Hundr's right and away from Bjorn's axe. *He can fight then.* It was the right thing to do, and Robert had known in an instant. He was away from Bjorn and behind Hundr now, which meant Hundr needed to turn and face him and halt the charge. He did that and heard a wet slap followed by a scream, and he knew that Bjorn had cut down a Lord of the Franks. Robert's sword crashed onto Hundr's shield, and the Duke raked his foot down Hundr's shin. He stifled a cry of pain and bullied Robert with his shield, and then turned a lunge into a slash, which Robert only just avoided by leaning back. Another warrior joined the fray and came at Hundr with an overhand sword strike, but this man was not as skilled as his Duke, and Hundr opened his throat and kicked him away and into Robert. The injured man bounced off Robert's shoulder, and the Duke flinched as blood poured down the sleeve of his fine tunic and onto his sword hand. The Duke snarled at Hundr, his cleanly combed brown beard looking like a pelt it was so shiny beneath a long nose and angry brown eyes.

"Back to back, fighting circle. We are out of time," Bjorn shouted. Hundr knew the manoeuvre. Bjorn wanted Hundr to back into him, and they would turn in a fast circle of slashing blades, but a shield would protect both front and back of each warrior. That would buy them a few moments before the Franks swarmed them. He backed into Ironside and once he felt resistance, he turned. A blade came for his face and ducked under the stroke, bringing up his own blade and burying it in a helmeted attacker's groin. Still moving, Hundr came around again and parried a thrust from Robert the Strong which jarred his arm to the shoulder. The Duke was red-faced, shouting at his men in his own language, no doubt urging them to kill the wild and blood-thirsty Vikings. Hundr kept moving and felt a bang on his mailed shoulder, but no pain, so the links must have held tight against the blow. He spun, and there before him was the other Frankish Lord, short fair hair above a long clean-shaven face. That unarmoured Lord attacked Bjorn's back as Ironside turned away, but he had left himself open. Hundr shouted as he struck the Lord in the ribs, close to Soulstealer's hilt, and Hundr sawed the blade back towards him with all his strength. The fair-haired Lord cried out in pain, the cry of a child screaming for its mother in the dark. Hundr had opened up his torso, and as he turned away again in the circle of death with Bjorn, he saw the Lord's ribs white against his tunic and shiny pale-blue of his entrails as they slopped onto the ground.

Hundr came around to Robert again, and knowing now that the Duke was a lover of battle, a fierce warrior who was not afraid to strike with his sword, he waited for that strike and took it high on his shield. Hundr broke away from the back-to-back formation and powered his shoulder into the bottom third of his shield so that the top pushed Robert's blade up and away, and the bottom rim smashed into the Duke's fine long nose crunching it into a lump of bloody offal. Hundr took a step back, and he heard Bjorn bellow and watched the big son of Ragnar lunge forward and thud his axe into Robert's chest. The Duke stumbled, and Bjorn roared in his face. He yanked on his axe haft, but he used such force that the blade stuck in Robert's sternum.

"Back Bjorn, he's dead. Back," Hundr said Bjorn jumped backwards, and the two edged backwards towards the church. Bjorn was laughing and shouting curses at the Franks. The enemy crowded around their three dead Lords. Their warriors running, pointing, and shouting but not able organise themselves into an attack. Hundr heard bows thrum again from behind him, and though he dared not risk a look behind him for fear of being charged in front, he knew Haesten's men kept the Franks from getting behind him and Bjorn. Hundr swallowed and blinked sweat from his eye. There were warriors beyond count massed before him now, at least a hundred men. They came on, without a leader but in a furious charge, their line ten men wide and ten deep. He and Bjorn could not hold against such numbers. They must surely fall. He closed his eyes. *Odin, I have sent you souls today. I charged and struck with the sword. Grant me a place in your mead hall.*

"Stop!" shouted a booming voice. It spoke in Norse, but the Franks held. Hundr kept moving backwards, taking quick but careful steps. Falling meant death, so the two warriors shuffled, not lifting their boots from the ground. The Franks halted their advance. Hundr saw their wolfish faces snarling, baying for his blood. He took two more steps back and felt the wide step of the church with his heel.

"We've made it," he said, but Bjorn had stopped and lowered his shield. He had stopped because his brother, Ivar the Boneless, strode in front of the line of Franks.

EIGHTEEN

Ivar the Boneless prowled in front of the baying Franks like a starving animal. He paced back and forth, a sword in each hand. His green cape was a clutch of colour in the grey cloudy morning. Ivar stared at Hundr and Bjorn, his face impassive, sword tips twitching as he prowled. Sten Slegyya faced the Franks. He held Warbringer, his double-bladed axe in two hands, and he somehow kept the howling Franks at bay.

The Franks massed in front of the church, where before they had been sleeping and quiet as night turned to morning, now they were a throng of shouting and spitting warriors, bristling with spear and sword blades. Their leaders were dead, Robert the Strong and two of their other Lords cut down in a savage attack. They wanted blood, but they were also leaderless. This was the rank and file of Robert's army, and whilst they wanted blood, they also needed orders. Sten barked an order and Ivar's warriors jogged from the west side of the church to make two lines between Ivar and the Franks, and there they made a shield wall. The Franks lowered their blades, faced now by the two lines of organised Viking warriors. They did not retreat, but Ivar's wild-looking plaid-clad Irish warriors were enough to keep them back, for now. Only a few of the Franks were professional warriors, the paid hearth champions of Robert and his Lords. Most were farmers and lay people called to arms in time of need to fight for their Lord.

Hundr watched his old friend Sten turn and come to stand with Ivar. Where Ivar was of average height and slight build, Sten was an enormous man. He was a hands span taller than Bjorn Ironside, and thicker in the shoulder. Hundr stepped back up onto the step of the church, but Bjorn didn't move.

"I killed their Duke. I killed Robert the Strong, Ivar. Have you come to help us get out of this bloody mess?" Bjorn said, and Ivar stopped pacing and raised one of his shining swords until it pointed at Hundr.

"I don't give a goats turd about Robert the Strong, or these mewling Franks. I want him."

Bjorn turned to look at Hundr. He chewed at his beard and then looked back to his brother. Hundr felt his stomach drop. It would be so easy for

Bjorn to hand him over. Hundr was sure that if Bjorn surrendered him to Ivar, that the Boneless and his two crews would march them out of the church and across the green fields, back to their ships. There was shouting and jostling amongst the Franks. Hundr thought they were no doubt trying to decide what to do now that their leaders were dead. Men needed leaders, and now they would argue to see who gives the orders. Which meant their discipline had crumbled, just as he hoped it would.

"The lad fought back to back with me, Ivar. He killed one of their Lords. He saved my life before. I can't just give Jarl Rune to you."

"Jarl Rune?" Ivar spat. "He's lied to you, Bjorn. My arse is more of a Jarl than that pup. Hundr is his name, a dog's name. He used to bail the bilge in one of my ships."

Bjorn turned to look at Hundr again.

"It's true, but I do command two ships. You have seen me fight, Bjorn. You and I fought out here alone, two against the entire army of the Franks. Odin and Thor are watching us, Bjorn," Hundr said. He did not know Bjorn well, but from what he had seen, Bjorn seemed like a good-humoured, open man. His men loved him, which meant he was fair. Hundr's only hope was to appeal to that fairness or face Ivar and the terror of the blood eagle.

"Ivar, I cannot just give the lad up. Look at how he fights. We can't just dishonour that in the face of the gods. He is a drengr."

"Piss drengskapr- shit on the way of the warrior. I'll come and take him if I have to Bjorn. I'll kill you all. I'll burn that church, and when you come running out, I'll cut you down. Before you die, I'll skin all your men alive and use their skins to make a new sail for my ship. Give him to me, give him to me!" Ivar was shouting, his face bright red and spittle flying from his mouth. He hopped from one foot to the other. Sten raised a hand for calm, but Ivar shook it away.

"You would kill me, brother?" said Bjorn, his voice flat and low.

"I'll kill you all, slowly. I'll send you screaming to Niflheim for eternity to wander in shame. Just give that turd with the dog's name to me."

"We are brothers, Ivar," Bjorn raised his hand and pointed at his brother, "We grew up together. We fought together. Our father was killed, and we swore..."

"We swore an oath that you neglected. I killed King Aelle. I cut the eagle on his back for what he did to our Father. He threw our father in the snake pit and you did not bring your warriors. I brought mine. Sigurd and Ubba came. You did not keep your oath. You went sailing and whoring with bastards and cowards."

Bjorn threw his head back and roared. For a moment, Hundr thought Bjorn would charge at Ivar, so incandescent was he with rage. But then the church door opened, and Haesten came out into the morning light, holding up a hand to show he came in peace.

"Lord Ivar, I am Jarl Haesten. Can we not talk awhile?"

"I want him. Give him to me. Then we will talk."

Haesten looked at Hundr, and his tongue flashed across his lips like a lizard, his quick pale-blue eyes searching Hundr's face. *He's going to give me up. He and Bjorn will walk away, and they will leave me alone under Ivar's knife.* Hundr knew at that moment there was only one path. The Norns laughed and spun their threads, and they had spun the threads of Hundr and Ivar's lives together. There could be only one way now. One of them must die. He couldn't let Bjorn or Haesten give him up. Maybe they wouldn't, but they probably would. They were Vikings. So, he pushed past Haesten. Hundr jumped lightly off the stone step and clapped Bjorn on the shoulder as he walked past. *He at least tried to defend me.*

"You have brought lots of warriors to kill me, Ivar. You fear me. I can see it in your face. I killed your whelp of a son, and I beat you. I took your sword and your reputation and made myself the champion of the North."

"You are a liar and piece of shit,"

"Let's fight again, you and I. Have your slave here," Hundr pointed at Sten. "make the square. We can fight here in front of your men."

Ivar grinned, his odd eyes twinkling. "Very well, I'll fight you. I'll kill you, and then I'll piss down your dead throat."

"If you win, you let Bjorn, Haesten, and their men leave."

"Agreed," said Ivar.

"If I win, your men must swear an oath not to attack us and swear allegiance to Bjorn."

"You won't win."

"Your men must swear, Ivar, or I won't fight you. We'll stay in that church and fight. You will lose more men than you can suffer. The Franks are at your back, and they want revenge for their dead leaders. They'll turn on you soon. Your men must swear."

"So be it. Make the square," said Ivar, waving a hand dismissively. The Boneless knew that much of what Hundr said was true. And Hundr knew Ivar did not consider for even a heartbeat that he would lose the fight.

Hundr stalked back into the church, closely followed by Haesten.

"Wait," said Haesten. Hundr stopped and

turned. Through the crack in the door, he could see Bjorn and Ivar talking, both gesticulating and pointing at each other.

"What is it? I just saved your life." Hundr said. He spoke harshly, but he didn't care. He had been sure the Jarl was about to surrender him to Ivar and his tortures. Hundr was all too aware that he was alone amongst the wolves. A man like Haesten didn't claw his way to wealth and power without leaving some corpses and betrayals along the way. It would be easy to give Hundr up. No one would protest. There would be nobody to bring Haesten to task. It would be the easiest thing in the world.

As he looked into Haesten's cold eyes, he remembered the lesson he had learned in Northumbria. His heart must be a stone and trust no one. Also, he knew now more than ever that he had to make his own luck. When he had left Northumbria, Hundr had been content to drift, wallowing in his sadness, not caring where or why he sailed. Now, he had a purpose. Kill Ivar. If he could get past that, if he could kill the greatest warrior in the north, then he would forge his own path and make his own destiny.

"I think you have just saved our lives. But we need to drag this out. If we can persuade Ivar to fight in the afternoon, as late as possible, then we might stay alive long enough for the army to arrive." Haesten's face changed into a pensive look, his white brows raised and his mouth open, jutting his angled jaw forwards.

"If Ragnhild and Kolo have made it out alive and found them."

"If they made it," Haesten allowed.

"Do you think Ivar will keep his promise?"

"He might if he kills you. But the Franks might not let him. Duke Robert is dead. You killed Ranulf, the Duke of Aquitaine, and Herve of Maine. Their leaders are dead, so their warriors might fade away and return to their lands, or they might fall upon us in a rage and run right through Ivar and his crews."

"So?"

"So, the fight must happen as late in the day as possible."

Hundr sighed. He supposed Haesten was right. The later the fight took place, the more chance they had of getting out of this alive. "I'll talk to Sten if I can."

Haesten nodded and placed his hand on Hundr's shoulder. "If we get back to the ships, I'll reward you for this."

"If I live. If I can kill Ivar the Boneless."

Haesten curled his lips into his teeth and smiled downwards. Hundr knew what he was thinking, that there was no chance Hundr could beat Ivar.

There weren't many men who could stand toe to toe with Ivar, to be within touching distance of the heat of his wrath and the ferocity of his anger. Ivar was fast and deadly. But Hundr had faced him before. He had stood against Ivar's wicked speed twice and lived to tell the tale. *I'll kill the bastard or die trying.*

Bjorn stormed into the church, huffing and muttering to himself. He dropped his shield, and the sound echoed around the high rafters.

"Brother or not, he shouldn't talk to me like that. I am Bjorn Ironside. He hates you, lad, and he's wicked fast. I don't want to see you dead, but I've seen no one beat Ivar with a sword."

Haesten stood up on a bench, and the Vikings turned to see what he would say. "They trapped us in a rathole, and now we have a chance to live. Bjorn and Jarl Rune killed two Dukes and a Frankish Lord. We are Vikings. We are drengr. Even with an entire army, they cannot defeat us!" he shouted, and the warriors inside the church chanted, *"Bjorn, Bjorn, Bjorn."*

Bjorn Ironside raised his fist to them in salute. Hundr spat on the floor. *Leave them their hero.*

Hundr walked outside of the church doors. It was strange to do that, after such ferocious fighting to keep the enemy out and the fury with which the Franks had assaulted the place. It was all calm now outside. He looked up at a grey, cloudless sky. Three small birds dived and chirped behind the lines of warriors and it was a still day, a calm day. Ivar's crews still stood as a barrier between the church and Franks, and Sten was there at its centre. Hundr took a few paces forward and sat on the church step, feeling the cold stone through his trews. His eyes were heavy again, and his body ached. The sleepless night, combined with that morning's fight, weighed heavily upon him. When he fought beside Bjorn, the tiredness had fallen away, and he had felt alert and alive. That was the joy of battle, the only time where Hundr felt truly happy. In that thin line between life and death, where men tried to snatch his life away or deal him a terrible wound, was where he found freedom. No thoughts of his loneliness or what had become of his life. Just the life and death struggle, his speed and sword skill coursing through his veins.

Sten strolled towards him, his axe leaning on his shoulder. Hundr rubbed his eyes with the back of his hand and yawned.

"You look tired," said Sten as he drew close.

"You look old."

Sten pulled a small skin from the back of his belt and handed it to Hundr. "Ale?"

Hundr took it and nodded. He took a long pull, and the cool liquid was soft and comforting as it snaked down his throat.

"I need some rest after this morning's fight. The Holmgang will be later this afternoon. Not before."

"Ivar is not a patient man. He wants to fight you now."

"You run along then and tell your master it won't happen until later."

"I did it for you and the others," said Sten, already bringing up old memories, quick to try and explain his betrayal in Northumbria. Hundr passed the ale skin back to him.

"You did it for yourself; to save your own skin. You wanted to be a famous warrior again, and here you are." Hundr said, but he knew it wasn't true.

"You would have all died there on that jetty. Ivar's men would have butchered you. It had to be that way, and she had to do it. For her people."

"She chose the wealthy Lord over the poor warrior, and you betrayed me. You both did." He knew that wasn't true either. Saoirse was a Princess of Ireland. Her father held a fragile peace with the Viking invaders of his land. Her marriage to Ivar's son Hakon made that peace possible. Once Hundr had killed Hakon, she had to go with Ivar once that became a possibility. She had to do it, or she would plunge her homeland into war, and her people would suffer. He knew these things were true, but knowing it and accepting it is not the same thing.

"She made the right choice. Ivar hates you. That hatred consumes him. He cannot sleep because you beat him."

"Not because I killed his son. Cold, arrogant bastard."

"You could run now. The church isn't surrounded anymore. The Franks are leaderless. You could just slip away through the back door or a window. No one would know until the Holmgang."

Hundr laughed mirthlessly. "Is that what you would do? Sten Slegyya, first over the wall at the siege of Paris, killer of Ketil the Black, Jarl Thorgrim Redbeard, and so on."

"No, I would not. But I don't want you to die."

"Don't make me laugh. I thought of you as a father, and you stabbed me in the back. Piss off back to your master and tell him the fight will happen when I say- late afternoon. I won't run away from Haesten and Bjorn and leave them to Ivar's savagery. I'm not a traitor like you." Hundr stood and walked back towards the church. His heart was heavy, and he cursed himself. Sten had come to him with kindness, maybe in some small way to make amends or at least have Hundr understand the reasons for his actions, and much of what he said was true. If Sten hadn't taken the tough decision to take

Saoirse to Ivar, then Hundr, Einar, Ragnhild, and the others would all be dead. He turned back to Sten. He regretted some of what he had said, but as he turned, he saw Sten stalking away. Hundr watched those broad rolling shoulders disappear beyond the line of Ivar's Irish warriors. It was too late, and so he went back inside to prepare himself to fight Ivar the Boneless once more.

NINETEEN

The Vikings and Franks gathered outside the church in a throng of heaving men, jostling for position to see Ivar the Boneless demonstrate his famous fighting prowess. Hundr cast his eye across the crowd, watching their hungry faces, knowing what they expected and what they wanted. They would bet shards of hack silver on the outcome, and few would bet against the champion of the Northmen to lose. Vikings were savage fighters, raised to it from the time they could hold a blade. They worshipped savage gods who urged them on to battle glorious feats of bravery. They were not like other men, not like worshippers of the Christ who preached peace. Northmen loved war, they loved treasure, and held above all things was the ritual of single combat.

Ivar, Hundr knew, had fought countless Holmgangs. He was famous for it. Hundr was not fighting to settle a dispute under Holmgang law, he was fighting for his life, and he was fighting to stop Ivar. If Hundr did not kill him, then Ivar would pursue him relentlessly. There could be no rest and no end to his ire. He sat in the church's shadow and noted it had drawn long, and the day drew on.

Sten stood at the far end of the square with his arms crossed. Two shields lay on the ground in front of him. Traditionally, the Holmgang square would be marked out with hazel rods, and the two opponents would fight within those limits. They deemed any man who stepped outside the rods the loser. Today, however, the square was made of Ivar's Irish warriors with the shields held in front of them. So, Hundr would fight inside a wall made of his enemy's shields. *As if fighting Ivar the Boneless wasn't daunting enough.*

Hundr spent the afternoon lying behind the altar, using a rolled-up cloak for a pillow. He had lain with his eyes closed, and flitted in and out of half sleep. Hundr did not enjoy sleeping. His dreams filled with memories of fiery blades burning the liquid from his dead eye, or being dragged along behind a horse across England's fields and briars, of betrayal, and of his mother. He did not welcome sleep, but he needed it. It had been a long two days of fighting, and he needed sleep to repair his body. He must be sharp to be any match for Ivar's speed. Rollo woke him mid-afternoon, and the grizzled warrior brought Hundr food and some water. It wasn't much, half an oatcake and a block of cheese, but Hundr was famished so the gesture was welcome. Rollo left him at peace to eat his meal, and again he welcomed that. The men inside the church also left Hundr to himself. Most likely, they didn't know what to say. What does one say to a man about to meet a great champion and fight for his life?

They called him to say that Ivar's men were gathered, and Hundr ignored that call for a while. He had taken off his mail and weapons to rest, but once he had eaten his food, he looked for his war gear to make ready for the Holmgang. Rollo came to Hundr with his mail draped over his arm.

"I've cleaned it for you. I scrubbed it with gravel from outside. It will shine now."

Another warrior approached with Hundr's swords. They gleamed with a blue sheen. Finally, Bjorn presented him with two shields.

"These are the best of those we have left," Ironside had said.

Hundr nodded thanks to the warriors. Those men were the elite of Haesten and Bjorn's crew, experienced warriors, each with a burnished reputation of his own. He felt their respect, and he thanked them. They hadn't accepted him; he wasn't one of them, but they respected his drengskapr. Hundr donned his gear and left the church to sit on the step again, and waited for Ivar and watched Sten across the square.

Haesten sat down beside him and smiled, his cruel slash of a mouth creating dimples in his hollow cheeks.

"Are you ready?"

"As I'll ever be."

"Can you beat him?"

Hundr shrugged. "I beat him before. But he is fast and vicious."

"Maybe it's enough that you are fighting him. You killed Lords of the Franks today, and you have a reputation, Hundr. We should not call you Rune anymore. You should be proud of your name, and if you go to Valhalla today, Odin and Thor will need to know what to call you."

"Do you think I can win?" Hundr asked. But he knew that was a foolish question. Haesten likely did not care if Hundr won or lost. Either way, he should be able to march to freedom, find his army and his treasure.

"I think you are brave and deserve honour. You won our lives back today, and win or lose, we will carry your saga and your reputation wherever we go."

Fine words won't matter much to a dead man, though. "I'll need a second. I don't want to fight with a shield, and Ivar probably won't either. But if he does, then I'll need a man to hold my shields."

"It would honour me to be your second," said Haesten, and Hundr thought that was no small thing, to have a famous and powerful Jarl as his second.

Hundr strode into the fighting square, with Haesten at his side, holding his shields. Hundr had Soulstealer at his waist and Munin strapped to his back. His mail shone bright, and he felt like a Lord of War. The gathered warriors roared and cheered, stamping their feet to create a thumping, rhythmic beat. There were Franks mixed in with the Vikings, men coming together to watch the most primal entertainment, two men fighting for supremacy. The Franks had lost all discipline now that their leaders were dead. They weren't an army anymore, just a rabble of armed men. Hundr sensed that their purpose had fallen away, and after they had watched this duel, he thought they would just fade away into the hills and forests, back to their homes and farms until the call to arms came again from some other Lord, Duke, or King.

The Vikings making up the perimeter square all held their shields up at neck level, so they created a wall of brightly coloured linden wood, and Hundr felt boxed in, like the square was tight and the air inside it cloying. He rolled his neck to loosen the tightness there and shook his shoulder muscles loose. As he did so, he looked at those painted shields. A raven here, a dragon there, gold and brown stripes adorned another. Vikings painted their shields and plaited their hair, and wore arm rings and gold chains. They were prideful men, proud of their warrior status, their wealth, and their reputation. Hundr felt the same. He had been so proud when Ivar awarded him two arm rings in Northumbria, rewards for his bravery and sword skill. He had lost those rings when Hakon Ivarsson captured him and put him to torture. Hundr breathed in and out, deep breaths to settle himself. His guts were a watery mess, and he had already pissed three times in the lead-up to the fight. He closed his eyes and remembered himself, as he was, aboard the Seaworm, bailing the bilge. Dressed in travel-stained rags, no weapons or wealth. His mind had been filled with hopes of glory and reputation. He had thought himself as a man then, but he was just a boy. Hundr exhaled and opened his eyes, setting his jaw and feeling for the comfort of Soulstealer's leather-bound hilt.

That boy was dead, long dead. He had died under Hakon Ivarsson's red-hot knife; it had singed away his spirit with the jelly of Hundr's dead eye, and his soul ripped away in Saoirse and Sten's betrayal. Even though it was, he now admitted, a necessary betrayal. The boy he had been was dead, and what remained was the warrior Hundr had always wanted to be. He was a scarred, one-eyed fighter, armed with two swords and a Brynjar chain mail coat. Only the wealthiest or most skilled warriors could own such expensive equipment. He pushed his shoulders back and saw himself as the gathered warriors saw him. He was a grim-faced champion, the man with a dog's name who fought like a Loki demon, the man who killed Hakon Ivarsson and who had faced and defeated Ivar the Boneless.

Despite his best efforts, Hundr's chest heaved as he felt himself working up into battle fury. He was standing alone, ready to face the Boneless, the champion of the Northmen. He looked around again at the leering bearded faces, and he knew there would not be many others who would fight in the square, alone, against so fast a brutal killer. Most of the men here would not be warriors who stood in the front rank, the lovers of battle. Most of the men here would wait in the rear ranks, shouting and making a show of bravery, but only willing to strike a blow at an enemy in flight. He cursed them all and spat in the dirt.

"Ivar, I am ready. Are you afraid?" Hundr shouted. He paced the square, grinding his teeth. He locked eyes with Sten, and the old warrior nodded in greeting. Hundr ignored him. A roar went up from the crowd, shields parted, and Ivar stalked into the fighting square, a long gleaming sword in each hand. He wore shining mail, his brown hair tied back from his handsome face with a leather thong. Ivar twirled his blades, and the warriors shouted themselves into a frenzy.

"No shields," Ivar called, staring at Hundr with his odd coloured eyes.

"No shields," agreed Hundr. He looked back at Haesten and nodded. The Jarl picked up the spare shields and paused. Fixing Hundr with a long stare. It was a look of support, and Hundr welcomed it. *At least there is one man who wants me to win this fight.*

"Now. Come to me, pup. Come and fight with Ivar," said the Boneless, and he flashed a wide grin, beckoning Hundr on with one of his blades.

Odin, grant me speed and strength. I will send you a great warrior for your Einherjar, if I can. But if I die, take me to your hall, and let me die quickly.

For a moment, the paralysing fear of the terrible wound that does not kill flashed across Hundr's mind. *What if he cuts off my arm, or I lose a leg? What if I take a blow to the head and lose my wits, to be left drooling and pissing down my leg?* Hundr drew his weapons, and in the feel and balance of those glorious swords in his hands, he pushed such thoughts away. They were not the thoughts of a drengr.

The two enemies circled each other, eyes locked

239

together and sharp steel poised. Ivar flicked out a sword tip, but Hundr took a nimble step back to avoid it. Ivar grinned again. Hundr feinted as though to strike high but brought his other blade in a low sweep aimed at Ivar's knees. But the Boneless leapt over the cut like a springtime lamb, and the crowd roared appreciation at his agility. Ivar stepped within Hundr's reach, keeping his own blades low at his sides. Hundr lunged at him, but the Boneless moved and dodged fast and lithe and then spun away, raising his blades to the gathered warriors who were now shouting out and calling out for their champion, glorying at his inhuman speed.

Hundr shook his head and rested a sword on each shoulder waiting for Ivar to finish his show.

"I killed your cowardly son, Ivar. I have his sword, and the one I took from you when I beat you. Are we dancing or fighting?" Hundr shouted and held up Soulstealer and Munin to show Ivar what he had lost. The smile fell from Ivar's face, and he charged. He ran towards Hundr and brought his two swords down in a thunderous chopping stroke, all hate and spite in the blow.

Hundr ducked under that wild swing, showing his own battle speed, and he brought a knee up hard into Ivar's stomach, and then spun to strike Ivar on the back with Munin's edge. The crowd inhaled as one. All the cheering ceased at that moment. The blow had not broken Ivar's mail, but the champion stumbled and turned to face Hundr. Ivar was white-faced and gasping to suck air into his winded chest. Now it was Hundr's turn to grin.

Ivar came on again, and their weapons clashed and clanged in a furious exchange of lunge, parry, and counterstroke. After a flurry of twenty heartbeats, they broke away from each other, both sweating and puffing from the exertion. The crowd remained silent, watching the two champions fight, knowing they were seeing the finest warriors displaying their skill at arms. Hundr felt a rumbling below his feet, like the earth itself was shaking. Then above the hushed crowd, he heard thunder, a low rumble at first, becoming louder and louder. The warriors around the square felt and heard it, too. They exchanged questioning glances with one another.

"Riders, Vikings," came a shout in the distance. A murmur of panic swept through the crowd. The square broke apart as men turned to see what was happening. Hundr laughed. He threw his head back and laughed from deep in his belly. For he knew in that moment that Ragnhild and Kolo had come. And they had brought the army with them.

All was chaos now as the gathered warriors fled, running in every direction. But it was too late. Hundr could see the horses charging through the town beyond. He could see their spears and axes rising and falling as they cut their way to the church. Hundr looked for Ivar and saw him screaming twenty paces away, where he had been jostled by the panicked crowds. The Boneless tore a spear from a fleeing warrior, and he spun. His eyes came to rest on Hundr, and Ivar bellowed with rage. He took a short step forward and launched the spear. It flew in a low arc, too fast for Hundr to react. He tried to block it with his swords, but it slammed into his waist, throwing him to the ground. He fell, and the pain exploded in his side and surged through his body. Hundr rolled to see where Ivar was, but he had disappeared into the maelstrom of horses and blades. Though he was wounded, Hundr laughed. He laughed with joy because Ragnhild had come.

TWENTY

Robert the Strong's army fled like startled birds before the Viking cavalry charge. The mounted warriors thundered through the town and around the church, and there were no enemy warriors to make a stand against them. The leaderless Franks simply ran for their lives. The Vikings cut many down as they ran, but most were just allowed to run away and melt back into the Frankish countryside.

Ivar's spear point broke through Hundr's mail and passed beyond his leather jerkin to tear a hole in Hundr's side. He sat shirtless, his back cold against the rough stone of the church wall. Hrist poured water over his wound, and he winced at the sting of it. Blood washed down his leg and onto the paving flags.

"Looks like I'll have to sew you up again," said Hrist, tutting as she searched for a needle and some gut thread in a pouch at her belt. "You have more scars than a warrior twice your age."

"Thank you, Hrist. I'll try to be more careful."

She was right, though. It had been Hrist who had sewed up his thigh and forearm where Saxon arrows pierced him on a Northumbrian Bridge. The shaft in his forearm had gone right through the shield boards and pinned the wood to his arm. She spent hours sewing and wiping away the blood that day. He also had heavy scarring on his face, his dead eye, and his back was a criss-cross of long white scars from where Hakon Ivarsson's men dragged him mercilessly behind a horse across the English countryside.

"You should. Or you'll be dead. You're lucky I'm here," she said and passed the needle point through a flap of skin close to his hip, "it's often not the wound that kills a man, but infection. If it isn't kept clean, it smells and a brave warrior dies sweating and screaming in his bed."

He grunted as she sewed him up. "Which is why they teach you Valkyrie to heal as well as you fight."

"To heal fools like you," she said and smiled at him, "so you can die in battle and go to Valhalla, or Thor's hall Thruthvangar. Odin will need men like you to defeat Loki when the day of Ragnarök comes."

He, Sten, and Ragnhild had rescued Hrist and Saoirse from the Saxons following an ambush in

Northumbria. She was a Valkyrie, just like Ragnhild. She'd been trained in Upsala to fight and
heal, to go wherever their high priest sent them,
wherever battle was fiercest, and to send souls to
Odin's hall. Hrist was a tall woman, slim in the
waist but broad in the shoulder. She had kind
eyes but a serious face. She was a killer, ruth-
lessly efficient with bow and axe. Hrist was quiet.
She never complained, and she was reliable. The
perfect warrior.

"Where is Hildr?" he asked. Hildr and Hrist were
always together. They lived, ate, and fought together, two sisters of the blade.

She huffed and shook her head. "Likely off with
Einar somewhere."

"With Einar?"

"Yes, with Einar. They are always together,
mooning over one another. If they aren't together, they are looking at each other and smiling like love sick children."

"Hildr and Einar, are you sure?" he said. Hildr
was a ruthless fighter, and Einar a grim sea Jarl.
Hundr knew them both, and couldn't imagine either of them falling in love, never mind falling in
love with each other.

"Yes, I'm sure. I have eyes," Hrist said, and
poked him in the ribs. Hundr started at the jab
and then cried out from the pain of his wound.
He laughed, and Hrist smiled at him. Einar had

245

often spoken of his desire to settle down and find a woman, and maybe Hildr was the perfect woman for him. She thought like him, like a warrior, and so would understand him more than some farm maid.

"I am happy for them."

"So, you fought Ivar. Again."

"Yes, we made the square, but you rode in right into the middle of it."

"Should we have waited then, until Ivar had killed you, before we rescued you, Haesten and Bjorn?"

"It's not finished. And it never will be until one of us is dead. There can be no peace and no rest until it's over."

Hrist shook her head and finished her sewing. She had Hundr stand and then wrapped a clean strip of cloth around his waist to cover the stitching.

"Keep it clean, and don't stretch. Or you'll burst the stitches."

He nodded his thanks.

"Still alive, then?" said a familiar voice. Ragnhild.

"Just about. So you and Kolo did it. You found the army."

"We got lucky. We crawled through the Franks

as they dozed. They never saw us. Then we headed back towards the river and blundered into Jarl Knut and his mounted warriors."

"I thought he'd gone, taking the horses after the treasure carts. Haesten was sure Knut had forsaken him."

"The bloody fool went too far North. By the time he looped back to hit the enemy flank, the battle was over. He missed the whole thing. So he was just on a hilltop, waiting for Haesten to appear. I don't think he knew what to do."

Hundr chuckled. It was easily done. In a foreign land and unsure of the terrain, Knut must have lost a sense of time. "Where's Kolo?"

"With Einar, riding the perimeter around this town to make sure Franks will not rally and come back to attack us."

"They won't. Where's Ivar?"

"We don't know. We couldn't tell the difference between Ivar's men and Haesten or Bjorn's men. So we didn't kill any Northmen."

"So he is here somewhere?"

"I don't think so. Most of the men have marched back to the river. They are nervous without their ships. Likely, Ivar and his crews are out there somewhere. You fought Ivar again?"

Hundr nodded and gazed out across the fields stretching off beyond the town and up into the hills. Sure enough, there was a long trail of war-riors tramping away, shields and weapons slung over their shoulders and heading back to the river. Now that the Franks were gone and no longer a threat, the Vikings were eager to secure the fleet. It was their lifeblood, their only way out of Frankia.

"Haesten and Bjorn?" he asked.

"They took most of the horses and rode away. We'll have to go on foot."

In the tumult of charging horses and scattering warriors, Hundr lay on the ground. The spear blow threw him down, and he'd crawled back to-wards the church and away from the chaos. At first, he thought the wound was serious and that he might die. The pain in his side overwhelmed him, and he lost consciousness, awaking to find Kolo sat next to him drinking ale. The big war-rior had grinned and laughed to see Hundr awake. By that time, the carnage had subsided, and all that remained of Robert's army was a scattering of dead bodies littering the town.

"Haesten will be hungry to find his treasure wagons. We should go, find the Seaworm."

Hundr put his hand on Ragnhild's arm. She looked at his hand, and then up at his face. Ragn-hild, too, had lost an eye, her face as ravaged by war as his own. No words passed between them in that moment of silent recognition. They had fought together on the edge of death many times, in that searing brutal forge of friendship where you become bonded to your shield brother or sister. Hundr trusted Ragnhild implicitly, and she trusted him. When Hundr had lowered Ragnhild and Kolo from the Church window, he'd known she would make it through the enemy and find the army. She would do it or die trying. Ragnhild had stormed Hakon's fortress in Northumbria to save Hundr's life, and in doing so, walked away from the life she loved. She had walked away from the Valkyrie order, from her sisters of the sword, to rescue him. As Hundr looked into her eye, he promised himself he would get her back to Upsala, the seat of her order. They may not take her back, but he would help her try. But first, he had to find and kill Ivar the Boneless.

The remnants of the Seaworm crew marched together through a field fenced for livestock, the animals themselves long since taken away and butchered by either the Vikings or the Franks to feed their warriors, and so all that remained as a reminder of their existence was short, clipped grass and turds. Ragnhild and Hundr both limped, she from her thigh wound and he from his wounded hip. Kolo walked next to Ragnhild. The two had sparked up a friendship on the journey to find the army. Blink, Bush, and Brownlegs marched ahead of Hundr with Hrist. The newer members of the crew made up the rear, and kept to themselves, marching quietly and keeping their distance from the original Seaworm men. What was most surprising, however, was to see Einar Rosti walking with Hildr. They kept themselves apart and talked in hushed voices, occasionally laughing and leaning into each other.

Hundr called to Bush.

"What is it? Don't tell me you have found someone else for us to fight?"

"He could start a fight alone in an empty field," said Brownlegs, and the men laughed.

"No," said Hundr, smiling at the jest. "What happened to Einar?"

"Him and Hildr have gone potty for each other. Blink saw them kissing the other day when we were off waiting to find out where you were."

"Kissing?" Hundr thought of Einar as the slab-faced warrior who had been his Jarl, implacable and prone to violence.

"They make a strange pair. Imagine what their children would be like?" said Blink.

"Probably pop out of Hildr with a full set of teeth and punch Einar on the nose," said Brownlegs, to more bouts of laughter.

"They have found each other, my friend. We all need someone to hold, a partner on cold nights," said Kolo, and Hundr saw him wink at Ragnhild, who then fussed at the neck of her chain mail.

The world has gone bloody mad.

"Where are the others, Guthmund, and the rest?" Hundr asked. He hadn't spotted them with Ragnhild's riders.

"Bastards don't march with us anymore," said Brownlegs and spat a curse. "They've gone over to Haesten's men. They aren't Seaworm lads no more."

"They swore an oath to Einar and I," said Hundr. They were oath sworn, and Hundr would hold them to that oath. He had shared silver and food with Guthmund and the new men. A man couldn't just walk away from an oath when he pleased or when circumstances suited.

They marched on until they came to the top of the valley summit, where days earlier, Haesten and Bjorn's forces had fought against Robert the Strong, and where Hundr had fought Ivar for the second time. The armies had churned the hillside to a muddy mess, and the casualties from that fight still littered the battlefield. They were bloated and stinking, crows pecked and tore at eyelids and lips, and most of the bodies had been stripped of anything of use. Locals no doubt darted in and out under cover of darkness to find some trinket or hack silver, even boots and jerkins they could re-use and at least take something of value from the conflict which tore through their homes.

Hundr could see the ship's masts in the river, and it was a sight to warm his heart. No Franks to bar their path. The sea could be only a day or two's gentle row downriver and away from Frankia. Hundr could see Bjorn's raven banner fluttering in the breeze, and Haesten's falcon flew alongside it. The warriors gathered and were resting, some lazing in the grass, and others stood in huddles, no doubt waiting for orders. Hundr saw Rollo and waved a greeting to him, but the look on Rollo's face made Hundr pause. Haesten's warrior looked to his left and then back to Hundr. His mouth turned down, and he was frowning. Hundr thought he saw a small but perceptible shake of the head, and a prickle ran down his neck.

"Something's wrong," said Hundr, and he stopped walking.

"What is it?" asked Ragnhild, and he saw Kolo searching the crowd ahead as though he had seen something amiss.

"I don't know. Keep together. Einar," Hundr called. The Jarl approached, trailed by Hildr.

"Keep the men together. Do we have any shields?"

"What's wrong?"

"How many shields do we have between us?" Hundr growled.

"Four or five."

"We might need them. Let's get the crew together."

Einar stared at Hundr, but seeing the concern on Hundr's face, he moved off to alert the crew and huddle them together, shields towards the front of their group. Hundr scanned the Viking crews, and it wasn't just Rollo who stared at him now. Most of the men were becoming silent and turning to stare at him. It was a strange sensation, like a wizard had cast a spell of silence over the Vikings, and it poured over them like a wave. He noticed Guthmund and Hrorik stood behind Rollo. Guthmund flashed a sickly brown-toothed smile in their direction. Hundr's chest was pounding, and the gorge in his throat rose. He took small steps backwards, keeping his eye forwards. He held his arms wide and pushed the crew back with him.

"What is it? Why are they staring?" asked Kolo.

Behind Rollo, the crowd parted; the warriors stepped aside to allow a group to march through. At the head of that group were Haesten and Bjorn Ironside, and so Hundr exhaled in a long blow of relief. But then Hundr saw a green cape flutter behind Bjorn, and as Ironside moved aside, there was Ivar the Boneless. Hundr's chest stopped, the world stopped. This was it. Bjorn and Haesten had turned against him at the last. He felt like he could vomit, and he grabbed Soulstealer's hilt to steady himself.

"There's been enough blood," said Haesten. "It's over, Hundr. Your crew can go free. They can keep your ships and their share of the treasure."

"Just you, dog. I just want you," barked Ivar.

"So, you found the treasure wagons then?" said Hundr. And he saw both Haesten's and Bjorn's eyes flick to Ivar, who smiled. He smiled a thin grin, but his eyes weren't smiling. Ivar's different-coloured eyes were like raven's eyes, shining and dark and cold, one deep and brown and one light blue. Hundr saw it then for what it was. Ivar must have stumbled across Haesten's wagons filled with the campaign's plunder, and that was his bargaining tool for Hundr's life. Bjorn would have accepted his brother willingly, Hundr and Bjorn had fought together and killed Duke Robert, Ranulf of Aquitaine, and Herve of Maine, and Hundr had thought them sword brothers. But Ivar and Bjorn were sons of Ragnar Lothbrok, and deep down, Hundr saw Ivar had sown the seed of shame in Bjorn's head when he taunted him for not joining the attack on Northumbria. All the sons of Ragnar had sworn an oath of vengeance against the King who had thrown their father into the snake pit, and all had fulfilled that oath, save Bjorn Ironside. Haesten would have allied with Ivar without hesitation. Once Ivar had the plunder, maybe he was aboard his ship and ready to sail away with Haesten's wealth. It could have happened that way or a hundred different ways. It didn't matter. The three were together now, and Hundr must die to keep that alliance together.

"We found them," said Haesten. His wide mouth a crescent of stern implacability. "Ivar's with us now. Throw down your weapons, and your crew can go free."

Hundr scratched at his cheek, and he nodded slowly.

"I see it means nothing to you both," he nodded at Bjorn and Haesten, "It means nothing that we fought and killed together. The blood of the Duke and his Lords is still on my blade. This is not drengskapr, and you are not drengr. I hope Odin is watching you and that he sees your betrayal. My Valkyrie, my priestesses of the All-Father, will pray to him and beg him not to let you into Valhalla. I condemn you to Niflheim to wander with the accursed for all time." Hundr spat at them, and Ivar laughed. Hundr continued to drift backwards, so there were twenty paces between him and Ivar.

"Your words are empty, and your Odin whores can die here with you. Einar Rosti, old friend. How are your guts?" said Ivar, and he laughed. Einar ignored the taunt. Hundr reached slowly, carefully, behind Ragnhild's back. She felt his hand there, but she did not show that recognition. He felt for her axe in its belt loop, and he slipped it free as Ivar laughed.

"Very well. I will give myself up if you allow my crew to live," said Hundr.

"Good, there's been enough blood spilled," said Haesten. But before he could speak further, Hundr let out a roar and hurled Ragnhild's axe at Ivar. *There's always more blood to be spilled.* It spun through the air, blade catching the sunlight as it spun head over haft. At the last moment, Ivar lived up to his name, and the Boneless swayed away from the flying axe. There was a spray of blood where its edge caught his face, but the weapon flew off behind him to thud into the chest of a warrior. That warrior fell to his knees, eyes wide in surprise, and Ivar clutched his hand to his face. Blood pulsed through his fingers as he bellowed his rage at the heavens. *You're not laughing now, you bastard.*

"Kill them, kill them now," Ivar roared, and across the mass of Viking warriors, they drew weapons in a clatter of steel and wood.

"Shield wall," Ragnhild ordered, and the four shields came to the front, linked to form a small wall, such a tiny wall of defiance in the face of a Viking army. "You've done it now," she said.

Hundr regretted the move the moment the axe left his hand, because in his pride and his hatred for Ivar, he had just condemned his crew, his friends, to death. The Vikings came on slowly, reluctantly even, as Ivar ranted and raved. Many of Haesten and Bjorn's men were unsure why a man who fought against them on the side of the Franks was now shouting orders. But with the sheer number of blades before him, Hundr thought they must die at the river's edge and in sight of the Viking fleet when from the corner of his eye, he saw movement and heard shouting. He looked to his right, and there, thundering across the field, was Sten Slegyya. The huge old warrior rode a black gelding and waved Warbringer around his head, and behind him, he led a string of horses. Sten Sledgehammer had come for redemption.

TWENTY ONE

A short, stocky Irish warrior from Ivar's crew in a plaid cloak ran for Hundr. He charged with a spear outstretched, and as he drew close, Hundr could see the rotten stumps of his teeth behind a grimy beard. That warrior was thrown five paces backwards and into his own men as Sten drove his mount through the Irishman as though he were made of straw. The Irish warrior yelped like a kicked dog, and Sten sawed at his horse's reins, bringing the war horse around to face Ivar's men. The gelding was trained for battle, and he snapped his teeth at one warrior's face and kicked his forelegs at another, cracking a skull with an audible snap. Sten twisted in the saddle and brought Warbringer down hard onto a helmeted head, and the double-bladed war axe cleaved his helmet in two, spraying Sten's gelding in thick gore.

"Get on the horses, now!" Sten shouted.

There was no time to delay. Hundr shoved

258

Ragnhild and Kolo towards Sten's line of horses, and he saw Einar lifting Hildr on the back of a grey mare. Hundr ducked under a horse's neck and came up with Soulstealer his hand and was surprised to see the oncoming warriors back off. He roared at them, but still, they did not come. They were facing Sten Slegyya, and Hundr supposed he had a fearsome enough reputation of his own. Most of those men had seen Hundr fight against the Franks or against Ivar himself, and he saw fear in their eyes. Even though there were so many of them, they feared to meet his blade. That fear, combined with the uncertainty of command, caused the Vikings to pause, and already behind him, he could hear that the crew were mounting Sten's horses as quickly as possible.

Hundr smiled at the horde in front of him.

"Who wants to fight? Where are the sword lovers, the spear Danes of reputation? Come, fight with the man with a dog's name."

"Get on, now!" he heard Sten shouting behind him. But Hundr drew Munin from his back and twirled his blades. A big man darted forward with a snarl, swinging an axe towards Hundr's neck, but he was slow. Hundr blocked the strike with both his blades and then sawed Soulstealer back across that brave man's throat and shouted in his face as blood sheeted down the big man's leather breastplate. Hundr looked for another warrior to kill, fury and rage pulsing through his veins. But an enormous fist grabbed the back of his Brynjar and Hundr felt himself hauled from his feet. Sten had grabbed him, and with his monstrous strength, Sten threw Hundr over his horse's neck. Hundr shouted his objection, but Sten kicked the horse into a canter and they raced away from the river and from the Vikings.

Hundr twisted and turned himself, and Sten slid backwards, so that Hundr held the reins and Sten sat close behind him. He heard a yelp from his left and twisted to see Blink had fallen from the back of Hrist's mount. She turned the horse to go back for him, but a clutch of Irish warriors were bearing down on Blink with their spears levelled.

"No!" Hundr shouted and wrenched the gelding around. The horse fought him, shaking its head and stomping its forelegs. He watched in horror as Blink rose to his knees and a spear burst through his chest, the point punching through the brown hard leather armour. Blink coughed a gout of blood and toppled into the dirt. Hundr cried out, and wanted to race hard to kill those men, but there were too many. Hrist yanked on her mount's reins, and her horse turned again. She dug her heels in, but the horse reared, and she had to hold on tight to avoid falling herself. Hundr flinched as an arrow soared past him to sink into the hillside ahead.

"Missile flight. Keep moving." Kolo said.

Hundr turned back to Hrist. She had her horse moving now, and she looked at Hundr with desperate wide eyes. He nodded to her as she caught up to him, and they spurred their mounts onwards and away from the pursuing warriors.

"Blink's gone," Hrist said, and Hundr saw tears rolling down her cheeks. He opened his mouth to reply, but the words died in his throat. An arrow slammed into her shoulder, above her collarbone. She tottered in the saddle and almost fell. Hundr leapt from the gelding and rolled heavily on the mud-churned hill, and then raced after Hrist. Her horse had slowed, and she was about to fall from its back, but Hundr caught her and leapt up behind her. He urged the horse on, and they thundered across the hillside and away from their attackers.

Once they were sure they had outrun any pursuers, the fleeing band came to rest in a clearing amongst a forest of elm and poplar. Ragnhild knelt by the river's edge, Hrist lay across her lap. The wounded Valkyrie's mouth, neck, and shoulders were covered in blood. It pulsed black and thick from the arrow wound in the space between her neck and shoulder and came red and flowing from her mouth. Hrist coughed again, spraying more blood on herself and spattering Ragnhild. Ragnhild rocked back and forth with her Valkyrie in her arms, and her shoulders

261

shook. She was crying, and Hundr himself felt a lump in his throat. He wished he could have wept for Hrist, she who had healed him so many times. She who had tended with care to any of the crew who had become injured. Hildr scooped up river water in two hands. She poured some into Hrist's mouth and the rest over the wound to wash away some of the gore.

"We've got to get the arrow out," she said.

"I know it. But I fear that when we pull it free, she will bleed out and be lost to us," said Ragnhild.

Hundr couldn't watch. His heart ached for Hrist, so brave in war and so skilled in healing. He took Munin from its scabbard and walked to her. He knelt and placed the blade in her hand. Her eyes flicked to him. They were wide, and the whites shivered like a forest deer. Her hand clamped around the hilt, and he held it there. *She must go to Valhalla.* He knelt down and kissed her forehead. She was sweating, and then it was too much, and Hundr gave himself over to pain. He fought to hold back tears and shook for her loss. Knowing there was nothing he could do beyond the skill of Ragnhild and Hildr, he walked away. He followed the riverbank, passing by Einar, Bush, and Brownlegs, who sat in silence, watching Hrist die and lamenting the loss of Blink, their sword brother. Hundr stumbled, his head reeling from the deaths of not just his crewmates but his friends. Hundr wrapped his arm around the white, gnarled trunk of a river birch tree and held on to stop himself from falling. He leant into the cold, rough bark and stared out into the water, where it bubbled and flowed around a branch, which had become snagged against some reeds.

"Hard to take, the deaths of friends." Hundr didn't need to turn to know Sten was behind him.

"Too much death. Too much blood."

"This is the life we chose. We know what it means to sail the Whale Road."

Hundr felt sick to his stomach as he thought of himself as a boy, his head filled with dreams of reputation and weapons and glory. He had dreamed of making his own way, forging his reputation in the world of the famous Viking Sea Warriors. His father's people had been such men, before settling in the East, and his mother's father had been a Jarl somewhere in Denmark. His nights had been full of the tales of Viking heroes, Odin, and Thor, and he'd thirsted for that life. *And now I have it. I have what I wanted, in all its horror.*

"I should have learned. You and Ivar both said it to me, on that day. The day you left me. You said take what you can, when you can, and trust no one. Ivar said the world is cruel, and you must be as cruel as it is."

"And it is."

"You got out of it, once. Maybe you were right."

"I did, and you know what happened. Kjartan Wolfthinker cursed my wife, and she died in agony, slowly, in our home. Then you and Einar came to the good brothers who took me in. They showed me kindness, and I lived in peace there. Einar came with blades and killed them all. You were there. You dragged me back in, and I broke my oath to my wife. I'll never be with her in her Heaven."

"So there's no way out?"

"Not for men like us. We are destined for Valhalla, just as Hrist and Blink were. This is the life of a warrior- men who don't want to fight stay at home to till the land and raise their families. We choose to pursue glory, reputation, and wealth. So it's no good complaining about it now. You have killed your fair share boy. You aren't the snot-nosed lad who bailed the Seaworm. You are the man with a dog's name, killer of Hakon Ivarsson, slayer of Ranulf of Aquitaine, and the man who bested Ivar the Boneless in single combat."

Sten was right, it was no good complaining about it now. Hundr had not thought about it like that before, but he was as much of a killer, as much of a Viking, as Ivar, Bjorn, and Haesten. Whilst he felt pain and sorrow for Blink and

Hrist, they had also killed and maimed and knew the risks.

"We are finished. Alone, without a ship. We're stranded here. The Franks will find us and kill us."

"We are not finished, lad. Have you learned nothing? We take what we need and what we want unless someone can stop us or kill us."

Hundr sighed. Surely there were no options for them now. Haesten, Bjorn, and Ivar would sail away. Hundr and the other surviving members of the Seaworm crew would be picked off and hunted by the Franks, who he knew would be watching somewhere, baying for blood and revenge for their dead Lords.

"I know you did what you thought was right," Hundr said quietly, still staring at the stuck branch as the force of the water tugged it one way, and the hold of the reeds pulled it back.

"It had to be that way, or you would have all died. She could never have forsaken her people."

"Is she happy?"

"No, she is not, but what does that matter? She is the daughter of a chief. Noble daughters do not marry for love. They marry for the betterment of their families and for their people. She is married to Ivar, and it keeps her people safe. Her sadness keeps her people out of a war with Ivar and his warriors. A war that would be fought in the homes and fields of those people."

"Is she in Ireland?"

"She is, and she is with child."

Hundr dropped to the ground. His love, Saoirse, pregnant with Ivar's child.

"I am sorry, Hundr. For everything," said Sten. The huge old warrior sat down on the damp earth next to Hundr. Sten put his arm around Hundr and pulled him close. Hundr felt the weight of that muscled arm and the warmth of it. He looked up at his old friend, into those pale eyes, and he could remember no one holding him like that since his mother had died. His mother's face came to Hundr's mind, as clear as if she stood before him, so kind and smiling. She was the only person in Novgorod who had ever shown him kindness. She was always warm and there with kisses to wipe away his tears. The tears of Velmud, scorned, teased and alone. Hundr allowed himself to lean into Sten's shoulder. He was tired, so tired. Tired of fighting and killing, of betrayals and backstabbing. He had always been alone. Hundr closed his eye to rest, and his head nodded, drifting into a sleep of exhaustion, his ears ringing with Hrist's blood spattered coughing and spluttering.

TWENTY TWO

*A crow cawed on his shoulder, its claws digging
into his flesh, and he reached up to feed it a scrap
of bread. Through his one eye, Hundr-Odin watched
his sons talking, his glorious sons Thor and Tyr.
Thor was burly and broad-shouldered, a thick braid
of blonde hair hung down his back, and a glossy
beard brushed against his thick chest. Tyr was taller
and more agile, warlike, and master of weapons,
looking so much like his mother, the giantess Hymir.
Thor held a long, shining rope in his hand. It shimmered gold and then silver. It was as light as a
feather, but there was not a stronger rope in all the
realms of the Aesir. For he had gone to the Dwarves,
deep in the kingdom of Niðavellir, and bade them
use their skill to craft a binding as soft as the gent-
lest ribbon but hardier than the strongest chain.
They had used their Dwarfish magic, gathering the
required items such as the breath of a fish, the spit of
a bird, and the sound of a cat's footfall, and forged
that mighty binding. Gleipnir was its name, and he*

267

watched now as Thor handed Gleipnir to Tyr, for Try was the cleverer of the two, and he would need all his wits to bind the ferocious Fenris-Wolf.

Hundr-Odin watched as the enormous wolf padded slowly and came to rest before his sons. Fenris-Wolf was of the brood of Loki and had grown to a monstrous size. Hundr-Odin shivered at the thought of the power in those jaws, but he was determined that the binding was necessary, even though it placed his sons in danger. The wolf must be bound and held fast, or it would ravage the world, and its power could well win the day at Ragnarök.

"You have grown large, cousin," said Thor to the wolf, his voice deep and rolling.

"Your reputation almost matches your size," said Tyr, standing straight-backed, his voice quick and clipped like the coming together of steel on steel.

"Almost?" growled Fenris-Wolf, saliva dripping from his monstrous teeth.

"Well, you are strong. But not the strongest being in all the worlds of the Aesir."

"Who is stronger than I?"

"Well, my brother here is widely held to be as strong as a mountain, and my father Odin is also very strong," said Tyr, taking and swinging Gleipnir around in a circle.

"I am stronger than you, Thor, and Odin," Fenris-Wolf said, standing to his full height and towering

over Thor, who laughed and crossed his arms.

"A test then. A test of strength. Let us see who is stronger," said Tyr, with a gleam in his eye.

"Yes, a test. What is the challenge? Shall we wrestle?" asked Thor.

"No, I have a better idea. This fetter is Gleipnir, wrought with Dwarfish magic. He who can break this fetter will be the stronger and have the greater reputation," said Tyr.

"Very well," said Fenris-Wolf.

"Good, you shall go first, cousin," said Tyr, and went to bind the great wolf.

"Wait a moment," growled Fenris. "How can I trust you, Tyr? What if this is a trap?"

"It's no trap."

"If it's no trap, then one of you must put your hand in my mouth whilst I am fettered. Once I break free, I will release the hand."

Fenris-Wolf was no fool, and Hundr-Odin watched as the rest of the gathered Aesir, those gods who shared the heavens, balked at the wolf's proposal. Even mighty Thor, God of Thunder and wielder of the hammer Mjolnir, hung his head and did not meet the wolf's challenge. Tyr stepped forward, bravest and most valiant of the Aesir, and without a tremble, placed his left hand in the beast's maw.

Thor took Gleipnir and bound Fenris Wolf and

then jumped backwards as the monster pulled and yanked at the Dwarf fetter. But he could not break free. And as the whites of the wolf's eyes showed beneath his mat of fur, he knew they had tricked him. Hundr-Odin watched in horror as the wolf's jaws clamped down, the razor teeth slicing and severing Tyr's hand in one bite; just as Tyr knew it would. Tyr himself had laid the trap, and he knew he would lose his hand as it went into the monstrous beast's jaws, but he did it anyway. For he was brave and determined, and to achieve the impossible requires the greatest risk. Tyr reeled away, clutching his bloody wrist, and the rest of the Aesir got to work, fixing Gleipnir to an enormous stone slab fixed deep into the ground. Tyr's bravery ensured that Fenris-Wolf would trouble the world no more. There, he would remain fettered until the day of Ragnarök.

Hundr awoke, his body and tunic drenched in sweat. For a moment, in that haze between deep sleep and wakefulness, he forgot where he was. Hundr's hand scrabbled in the dry grass, searching for his weapons. His head shot from side to side in a heartbeat of panic. Then he saw the river before him, babbling and flowing relentlessly on its seaward journey. He heard the breeze rustle the leaves in the boughs above him. His side throbbed, and Hundr pressed his hand against the wound, and it came away spotted with blood. He pulled off his mail and his tunic and leant over the river to splash its cool water on his face and torso. With a groan, he untied the dressing Hrist had applied and rinsed the fabric in the water and washed the raw and jagged flesh with the cloth. He re-applied the dressing and drank deeply from the river. He pulled his tunic and Brynjar back on, secured Soulstealer's fleece lined scabbard at his waist, and slung Munin across his back.

Hundr breathed deep, sucking the Frankish air deep into his lungs and exhaling long and slow. Where before there was sorrow, sadness, and doubt, he expelled those thoughts and replaced them with determination and decisiveness. Hundr felt ready. There was no more time for sorrow and regret. Now was the time for bravery and to do what must be done, to do as Tyr had done. Hundr swore an oath to Thor and Odin, an oath that from that moment on, he would no longer allow sadness for himself and grief to cloud his judgement. He would run from his enemies no longer. He was a warrior of reputation, and from now on, he would bend the world to his own will.

Hrist lay on the grass, her bright eyes open and glassy. Streams of watery blood ran from her mouth down her cheeks where she had coughed away the last of her life. Ragnhild and Hildr stood over her, holding hands and staring at their dead Valkyrie sister.

"Hrist was brave, and she died like a warrior.

She wouldn't have had it any other way. She will be in Valhalla now, feasting with the other heroes. When it is our time, she will save a place for us at a bench, and we will drink and fight alongside each other once more."

Ragnhild flicked her head up and stared at him, her one eye shaking and her cheeks stained with tears. She nodded, for she knew that was true. Hrist was gone, but she had died in battle, which was every warrior's dream.

"We will send her off like a battle queen. Come, help me make a bier for her," said Hundr, and he picked Soulstealer from her dead, icy fingers, and went to cut branches on which to place her body. They all helped and cut sturdy boughs. The Seaworm crew lashed the branches together with the string from Hrist's bow, and then laid her body upon the bier. Ragnhild strode into the river and waded in until it reached her chest. She dragged Hrist's' body out into the deepest part of the river flow and pushed it away. It flowed on safely downriver, away from the banks where they hoped her body would sail on into the Whale Road.

Ragnhild and Hildr sang a prayer to Odin for Hrist and Blink. Both fine warriors and good friends, gone now into the afterlife. Hundr felt the sombre mood overtaking him again, but he forced those feelings away. The time for sadness and thoughts of the past was over.

"Come, we must talk. Our friends are gone, but now we need to decide what to do next, how to move forward."

Hundr leant against a sprawling alder tree, below a pale-blue sky, forcing its way through cracks in the heavy grey cloud covering. Ragnhild, Einar, Bush, Kolo, and Brownlegs stood in a circle around him, along with Sten. The others found it easy to welcome the old warrior amongst them again. He had saved them from Ivar's wrath and Bjorn and Haesten's treachery.

"So, what do we do?" said Brownlegs. He looked at Einar, and then at Hundr. Einar was a sea Jarl, promoted to that position during his service with Ivar. Hundr still thought of Einar as his Jarl, but since Ivar had wounded Einar during their fight in Northumbria, Einar had taken a backward step. He was not the Einar of old, which was a difficult thing to face and confront. Before Frankia, and whilst they sailed across Saxon and Frankish coastlines raiding for supplies and silver, Einar had command of the Seaworm and the sailing of the ship, but Hundr made plans and took control of all things battle-related. Hundr watched the crew, and he saw Brownlegs looking from him to Einar, uncertain of where to look for leadership. Einar stood with Hildr, which is where he always was these days, and there was a different air about him. Hundr suddenly realised that he had not seen Einar strike a blow in anger

273

since the day he'd fought Ivar. It was understandable. He had suffered the horrifying pain of the grievous wound that does not kill on the battlefield, and but for the skill of Hildr and Hrist, he would have died a long, slow death; a warrior's biggest fear. Einar caught Hundr's eye, and the Jarl's flat slab face gave a slight nod. A small gesture, but enough to give his blessing for Hundr to assume command, to take full responsibility. Hundr nodded back. He loved Einar, and that moment passing between them was the passing of a mantle, a changing of the guard. Like a father handing over his farm or his prized weapons to his son and heir. Einar had taken Hundr in on a rain-soaked stinking pier in Jutland when he had nothing, and he would never forget that.

"We don't run anymore. Ivar won't give up until we are dead. Even now, he will search for us across these hills and forests. We should have faced him down that day in the river before all of this began. Since then, we have delayed the inevitable. We must find the courage and a plan to put that sneaky double-crossing bastard in the ground," said Hundr.

"You are right. He won't stop. But how can we go after him?" said Bush, throwing up his hands.

"We are only a few, and he has two crews. Now he is with Bjorn. They have over twenty ships between them. We've lost the Seaworm. we have nothing," said Brownlegs.

"We have our weapons, and we have some silver between us still," said Ragnhild, patting the pouch at her belt.

"We have our honour as warriors, my friends," said Kolo.

"That's all well and good," said Bush, "but what are we going to do? There'll be Franks crawling all over this land, looking to pick off Viking stragglers. We have to go somewhere, do something."

"You are all right in what you say," said Hundr. "We will go back the way we came, watch them, see what their plan is for loading the treasure and getting the ships upriver. There are many long hundreds of warriors and ships to load up. They can't all sail at once."

"You want us to go back? Blink is dead, Hrist is dead, and you want us to go back?" Bush shook his head and looked at the ground in despair.

"We go back," said Hundr, more firmly this time. "There will be an opportunity. A straggling ship, treasure unguarded, horses left behind. There will be a chance for us to seize something."

"So say we find our way onto a ship or get some horses. What then?" asked Brownlegs.

"Then we hunt Ivar, and we kill him."

"With just this handful of us?"

"Yes. Who better to get it done than us?" Silence descended on the group, and Hundr let it sit there. They looked at each other, searching for confidence or challenge for Hundr's words. He let a few moments pass.

"Sten, you have been with Ivar. Where will he go now?"

"Ireland, more than likely. To check on his lands there, his eldest son minds those holdings, but Ivar will want to make sure it is safe."

"Not England?"

"If anywhere it will be Ireland. He won't give up on you though. He hates you."

"You don't think he will leave now?"

"No, I think he's out there scouting these hills and valleys right now. He knows you're out here, with just a handful of warriors. He won't leave Frankia until you're a corpse, lad."

"So, first, we need Ivar to think we are dead," said Ragnhild.

"Then, once he has given up the chase, we go after him."

"All seven of us," said Brownlegs, and they all chuckled mirthlessly.

"Let's take it one step at a time," said Hundr. "We go now and watch the army, see how and if they are preparing to leave. Let's see if there are opportunities there. Then we'll worry about how to make Ivar believe we are dead. And hope he doesn't find us first."

TWENTY THREE

Hundr, Kolo, and Einar lay belly down on a bed of damp pine needles. They had made the long ride up to the largest peak in the area, a high rise to the south of where the moored Viking ships rested in a river's bend, and to the southwest of the town where Hundr had fought at the church. A grove of dark pines gave them cover, atop a ridge of rock running down and dying away into a gorge where the escarpment turned north-wards. They lay on the edge of that peak, and before them, the entire Breton valley opened up. Hundr could see the cross atop the church where he had fought alongside Bjorn, but more import-antly, he could follow the long wide meander of glistening water where it cut through the deep greens and browns of a dense forest to where the Viking ships lay at a place where forest gave way to fields cleared for livestock and farming. Only, not all the ships were still. A long line of drakkar warships ambled down the river like a line of ants crawling across a log on summer's day.

"Can you see their banners?" Hundr asked, straining his eyes to make out the symbol fluttering from the high masts.

"Too far away," said Kolo. " I can't see a Raven, but I know they are Bjorn's ships."

"How can you be so sure?" asked Einar, pushing himself up to a seating position. "Bloody needles are digging into me," he grumbled, itching behind his Brynjar.

"I know them. I have sailed alongside them for many months. Trust me, my friend. They are Bjorn's ships."

"So it looks like Bjorn and Haesten are going their separate ways. They must have shared out the takings," said Einar. "I think Sten is right, though. Ivar won't leave until he has your head. Mine too, I'd wager."

"He's right enough," said Hundr.

"So, what now?"

"We wait and watch."

"For what?"

"For Ivar."

They kept to their position, watching Bjorn's fleet row at a relaxed pace upriver. Hundr counted twenty ships, along with eight hundred warriors leaving Frankia. Which left Haesten with a similar number of ships and men, and

Hundr watched and thought, and a plan took shape in his mind, a plan to get Ivar out of the way and back on the seas. But to do that, he must be brave, and he must use cunning.

The afternoon waned, and Hildr brought some food to the watchers. She had caught two birds with her bow, and on the other side of the hill, Bush had got a small fire going. He had made sure the smoke couldn't be seen from the side of the hill leading down to Haesten's camp. Hildr gave Hundr, Kolo, and Einar some strips of warm meat along with nuts and berries foraged from around the hilltop. It was a welcome meal, and the three warriors tucked in hungrily. Whilst they ate, Hildr leaned against a pine trunk and, using her hand to shield her eyes from the sun, which was now low in the sky, she looked across the valley basin.

"What's that?" she said, pointing to the east of their position. Hundr followed her finger to a series of meadows, a patchwork of yellows and browns, where riders picked their way across the fields. Hundr stood, and he knew this was the opportunity, the time to be decisive.

"It's Ivar, has to be. He's looking for us, and he's going away from Haesten's camp."

"So, what use is that to us?" said Kolo.

"I'm going to talk to Haesten, and you're coming with me."

Hundr and Kolo rode towards Haesten's warriors. They pushed their mounts hard down the hillside and through the woodland to get to Haesten before, and in case, Ivar doubled back to the Viking camp for the night. Haesten's camp was a makeshift stockade of sharpened staves, pointing away from the river. A line of warriors guarded it, and Hundr and Kolo approached slowly, arms held out wide at their sides to show they came in peace.

"You've got some nerve showing your face here," growled a grizzled, red-faced warrior in a faded leather breastplate.

"Tell Jarl Haesten I am here to talk with him," said Hundr.

"Who do you think you are? What makes you think he will know your name?" said the warrior belligerently.

"You know my name. All you men here know who I am. You saw me fight back to back with Bjorn Ironside. You saw us kill Dukes Robert and Ranulf. You saw me fight Ivar."

"I saw you," chirped a young warrior.

"Lord Ivar wants your head. Maybe there's a reward?" said the red-faced warrior.

"Get Haesten, or you and I can make the square," Hundr growled. The warrior straightened his back and puffed out his cheeks.

"Alright, I'll tell him- no need to lose your temper. I'll tell him the man with a dog's name is here. And you, Kolo."

"How are you, Gilfi? How's your foot, my friend?"

"It hurts, Kolo. It's a curse the gout is." He nodded at Kolo and marched off. Moments later, he returned and waved Hundr and Kolo into Haesten's camp.

The warriors inside the makeshift stockade were not in a state of high readiness. They sat together in groups, drinking ale, playing knucklebones, and the air was filled with the hum of conversation, punctuated here and there by outbursts of laughter. Haesten strolled towards them with his short quick-stepped gait, flanked by his trusted captain Rollo and his brother Erik. It surprised Hundr to see the Jarl not wearing his mail. Such was the confidence in the Viking army that they were not in any way ready to fight. Haesten wore a fine brown tunic with a thick gold chain coiled about his neck like a rope. He had a flowing cloak thrown over one shoulder and his glorious silver and gold studded belt around his waist.

"Well, well. I didn't expect to see you again," Haesten said, the slash of his mouth always pointed downwards, making it hard to tell if he was smiling or frowning. His clever eyes searched Hundr carefully, and he came to a stop, tucking his hands into his belt.

"Ivar is abroad, hunting," Hundr said. If his plan had any chance of working, it hinged on Haesten's opinion of Ivar.

"He is. You cut open his pretty face with that axe throw. He hates you even more now if that's possible given how much he hated you to begin with."

"You are allied with him?"

"I wouldn't say that, as such," said Haesten, and the corners of his mouth twitched. Which was the sign Hundr was waiting for. He had hoped that Haesten saw Ivar more as a rival than an ally. No doubt Ivar had cajoled and shamed Bjorn into taking up the fight against the Saxons and had, therefore, driven a wedge between Haesten and Bjorn. Their strength was the size of their combined fleet and army, which they had used to make themselves rich in the warm south seas, and now again in Frankia. Now that Bjorn had sailed away, Haesten was not as powerful, and whilst twenty ships and eight hundred men were still more than some kings could muster, his power was halved.

"I come to you for your help, Lord. I have a proposal that might work for both of us."

"Go on."

"Ivar draws Bjorn away from you. He shames his brother into joining the sons of Ragnar in their war against the Saxon Kings."

"Bjorn has gone, that's true."

"Sailing for England?"

"To join his brothers Sigurd and Ubba there."

"You had a long forty ships and fighters to crew them. Now you have half that number. You could not, for example, fight the war you just fought for Duke Salomon with those numbers."

"Careful," growled Erik. Hundr smiled at him.

"That's also true," Haesten allowed. His mouth set firm, he pushed his shoulders further back. "But I am rich now, richer than I was when I left your home, Kolo."

Kolo inclined his head, "You were a great Sea King then, Lord. None of the Muslim fleets could stand against you."

"What are you saying, that we're finished? Have you come here to insult us? You two masterless men, a slave and the man with a dog's name?" barked Rollo, and he spat at Hundr's feet. Haesten remained impassive. He didn't stop Rollo from insulting Hundr and Kolo, but nor did he show he agreed either.

"No, it is no insult to speak the truth," said Haesten.

"What's your point then, turds. I grow tired of your yapping, like two puppies without a master. Maybe we should chuck you both in the river?" Rollo said, nodding to himself as though his idea pleased him mightily, and Erik grinned along with him.

"Like a game of tafl, there are lots of pieces of the board at the moment..." Hundr began.

"Tafl? Don't make me laugh. Let's get you two in the river," Rollo interrupted.

"You talk too much, little man," said Kolo. Hundr raised his hand to quieten his friend. Rollo was trying to antagonise them. The spiky little warrior acted like the dark side of Haesten's inner voice. He gave voice to the challenge and the warlike nature of Northmen, where Haesten was so calm and thoughtful. Haesten allowed Rollo to speak in that way. Hundr thought the Jarl enjoyed Rollo's abrasive manner, and it helped Haesten. It put men on the back foot, caught them off guard, and allowed Haesten the upper hand. He could think calmly and clearly where his opponent in that discussion, usurped by Rollo, was agitated and distracted.

"What are you going to do about it?" Rollo challenged, smiling. The dark space between his missing front teeth cavernous and the scar across his nose twisting.

"There are too many pieces," Hundr said, ignoring Rollo. "The Ragnarssons are making themselves Kings and Lords in England. Ivar already holds the most valuable part of Ireland for himself. Here in Frankia, we might have defeated Robert the strong, but eight hundred men are not enough to challenge King Charles the Bald. Then at home, in the north, we are all warlike, and the lands are full of ruthless and powerful Jarls. To the east, in my homeland, the descendants of Viking warriors rule the great cities, like Novgorod."

"So, what are you proposing?" Haesten said, and he sighed and rubbed the bridge of his nose. *Better get to the point.*

"I want to help you create a space on the board, remove a few pieces."

Haesten dropped his hand and stared hard at Hundr through furrowed brows. "How?"

"I want you to give me a ship and ten men. With that, I will wipe Ivar off the board. If I take away Ivar and his warriors, then it weakens the Ragnarssons. They will need to keep their forces in Northumbria to hold on to the lands they have won, giving you the option to strike at either of the rich lands of Wessex or Ireland."

"Wessex?" said Haesten.

"It's the breadbasket of the Saxon Kingdoms. It makes the lush greenery and fields here look like parched scrubland. It's the richest Kingdom in

England."

"So, how are you going to remove Ivar? He has two crews, and an army in Northumbria, and maybe another one in Ireland. What have you got? A slave and a few crusty whores?" said Rollo, and he smiled thinly at Hundr and Kolo, hoping he was chipping away at their resolve with his harshness.

"I'll make him think I'm dead, and then he'll leave. Ivar will sail from here around the south coast of Wessex, around Cornwall, and up to check on his holdings in Ireland. I will attack him there and draw him out to fight. Then, I'll kill him and piss on his dead bones."

"How will you draw him out?" said Rollo, blowing his cheeks out and mimicking Hundr's eastern accent.

"I'll hit him with harsh attacks and barbs. I'll strike at him to throw him off guard and goad him to violence."

Rollo laughed and inclined his head at that riposte.

Haesten nodded his head slowly. "I'll give you Rollo here and ten good men. Bjorn did not take your ships, but if you want your ruse to work, then you must leave them here. Dead men don't sail off into the sunset. I'll give you one of mine."

"And what would you like in return, Lord?"

Haesten smiled, his grin wide and broad. "You will swear an oath to me," he said, "once you have killed Ivar the Boneless, you will come to Wessex and join me there to fight the Saxons."

Hundr's heart sank. He knew there would be a price, that there was no way Haesten would help him and risk the wrath of Ivar without asking for something in return. If Hundr was successful and killed Ivar and disrupted the Ragnarsson forces in England, there was an opportunity for Haesten. With the English kingdoms distracted by the Great Ragnarsson army and that army weakened, there was a chance for Haesten to sail into Saxon England and cut his own swathe of blood and glory and make himself richer. Maybe even win a kingdom for himself. With this oath, Haesten was securing himself a crew of killers. Hundr, Ragnhild, Einar, and Kolo were all warriors with reputations, and adding them to his forces could only improve his chances of victory in Wessex.

"Agreed, Lord," said Hundr, and nodded his head in thanks. Rollo smiled at Hundr, for Rollo knew he would get a chance to fight, and there were few warriors who loved battle as much as Rollo. "I need those men now if I am to convince Ivar that I am dead. Also, I want those two on the crew." He pointed to Guthmund and Hrorik, who skulked behind Erik and the other leaders. The newer members of the Seaworm crew had deserted Hundr and the older crew. They had turned their cloaks at the first opportunity, like the oathbreakers they were.

Later that day, riding hard through a bluster of spitting rain and wind, Hundr, ten of Haesten's men, and the Seaworm crew headed back to the church, where they had fought so desperately against Ivar and the forces of Robert the Strong. Corpses still littered the battleground, swollen now and stinking. The local Frankish peasants were still too afraid to strip and rob those fallen warriors for clothes, weapons, and armour. Hundr's plan was grim, but he knew that to get his chance to kill Ivar he must be brave, cunning, and of iron resolve. And so they dragged ten of those fallen warriors into the church, laying them at the windows and doors. They ran off the Christ Priests and did what the Franks should have done during the siege, but for their piety. They set the grey-gold thatch of the church aflame, and, standing in the town watching the huge building crackle and roar with flame, Hundr thought about how he would tell Einar about the oath he had sworn to Haesten. When leaving Northumbria, they had agreed never to swear to another Lord again, to always be the masters of their own destiny. But to be free, Hundr had to kill Ivar, and to kill Ivar, he needed Haesten's help.

"Over to you, Rollo," said Hundr. They would

ride back to Haesten's camp, and from there, Haesten would send warriors to tell Ivar that he had captured and killed Hundr in that church. Ivar would rejoice and dance on the ashes of the burned warriors. Hundr would set sail with his crew and Rollo's men. Once at sea, Hundr would give the Norns what they wanted. He would follow the thread of his destiny and lure Ivar out to fight.

TWENTY FOUR

Einar's back tweaked as he hauled a dead Norseman over the side. He winced and rubbed at the small of his spine, and the corpse splashed with a flat plopping sound into the swell of a grey sea beneath a dull metal-coloured sky. Einar had not killed that man. He had still not struck a blow in anger since Northumbria. Hundr had killed him with an axe blow to the face, leaving the warrior's skull a bloody mush of bone and torn flesh. Hundr and the crew killed with brutal efficiency since they arrived in the Irish Sea to begin hunting Ivar's ships, prowling up and down the coast to run them down with sailing skill and savagery. This was the third of those ships, shorter than their own ship, the Sea Bear, borrowed from Haesten. Ivar's captured ship had a fine oak keel, and her maker had cut her clinker-built hull from birch planks. She was a Northman's ship, crafted with love, care, and skill.

Einar stretched out his back and leant against the side. He kicked his boot at the horsehair caulking between the overlapped clinker timbers; she was freshly caulked, and the bilge was dry of water, so not only was she a fine ship but also well cared for by a proud captain. Einar wasn't sure which of the dead warriors was that captain, but they were corpses now, and so it didn't matter. He watched Hildr collecting blades and making a pile by the mast. They had taken some fine mail coats from the three ships, as well as axes, short swords, knives, and a few helmets; all items of value. Hildr looked at him and smiled. She had a crooked smile, her mouth turned up slightly in one corner, and he smiled to himself to see it. During the fight to kill this crew, Hildr had thrown herself into the violence with brave ferocity, as she always did, but it was unbearable for Einar to witness. At every clash of blades and shields, he thought they would take her from him; that she would be killed so soon after he had found the warmth of her love. They had spoken together of his dream of settling down, of finding some land, and at first, she had laughed, thinking only of her oath to serve Odin as a warrior of the Valkyrie. But she had warmed to the idea. She had, he had told her, sent enough warrior's souls to Valhalla and had carved her own place there, and so why not live out her later years in peace and enjoy life without being surrounded by death.

On a chilly night at sea this past week, where they huddled together under a sail dragged across the ship to keep off a shrill night squall. Hildr asked Einar if he had lost his ferocity when Ivar's blade bit deep into his stomach. Einar flinched from the question but then admitted that he had. All that pride, ferocity, his enjoyment in the thrill of violence had flowed out of him in the blood which seeped out of his stomach and down Ivar's icy blade. Hildr had pulled him close and told him it might return, that love for fighting and the clash of one man's strength against another. But he knew it wouldn't. He felt it deep within him. That fire in his soul that had earned him his name, Rosti, the brawler, had been taken from him and would never return.

"Let's get moving," barked Hundr from amidships. Hundr was now a grim-faced Viking war leader. The boy he had picked up in the Jutland peninsula was long gone. Einar remembered that day, at a quayside stinking of untreated wool and shit. A scruffy broad-shouldered youth, little more than a boy, had approached him asking for a berth aboard Einar's warship Seaworm. He would usually have sent such a lad away with a clip around the ear, but there had been something about that boy, a glint in his eye. That meeting had changed Einar's life, and he wondered now, looking at the man that boy had become, had he made a terrible decision that day?

Before Northumbria, and before Hakon Ivarsson had conspired with Jarl Guthrum to turn Ivar against him, Einar's path was laid out before him. At that time, Einar served Ivar and was Ivar's most trusted captain. Ivar had made Einar a sea Jarl, and had promised Einar a land jarldom, which meant land and wealth and warriors of his own. That dream had died when Ivar cast him out, and the root of that betrayal was Hakon's jealousy of Hundr's relationship with Hakon's wife.

"Tie her up, good and tight lads," said Rollo. They would tie this newly captured vessel to the Sea Bear and tow her into the safe spot they had found down the coast where the other two of Ivar's captured ships lay moored.

"That should stick a poker up Ivar's arse," said Sten, who stood with Einar.

"He'll be hopping mad," Einar replied. "He still has another five left, though."

Upon arriving in Ireland, they had spent days watching Ivar's forces' activity around the port city of Dublin, which was Ivar's base in Ireland. It was a growing trade town, with a prosperous slave market and also a more general merchant and trader market. Sten had predicted that Ivar would return to Ireland before returning to his brothers and resuming the campaign against the Saxons. Much of Ivar's wealth was tied up in Ireland and held under the stewardship of his elder son, Ivar Ivarsson.

"Most of his men stayed with Ubba and Sigurd. Nevertheless, five ships mean we're outnumbered."

"Will he fight?"

Sten looked at Einar with a raised eyebrow, and Einar knew the moment the words left his lips that it was a stupid question. Of course Ivar would fight. He would know now that someone was targeting his ships off the coast, and he would worry it was his reluctant Irish allies, who had been his most bitter enemies before the union between his family and that of Princess Saoirse. But the Irish were poor shipbuilders, much like the Saxons in that regard, and Ivar would fear that some Viking Lord looking to make a name for himself had come to test him, and Ivar's pride would be spiked.

"Let's hope he comes out soon then. Let's get this bloody fight over with once and for all."

"Did he treat you well, Ivar?"

"Of course, he is a good Lord, a good ring giver. You know that better than most, Einar. That's why his men love him."

"Do you ever wonder what would have happened had our paths never crossed, had I not taken the man with a dog's name into my service, or we had sailed past your monastery?" Einar remembered that day as clearly as he remembered his last meal. He had led the Seaworm in a raid into Western Northumbria where they hoped to find some easy plunder. Einar had been on a mission for Ivar to his lands in Denmark and, on the return voyage, hoped to enrich himself. They had raided a plump Christ Monastery, but Sten had been there. Sten Slegyya, a figure from legend.

"There's no point thinking like that, Einar. The Norns weave our destiny. We are all subject to the whim of the threads they spin."

"So you have completely given up on the Christ God now?"

"The day they took Hundr, you were there. I killed that day and broke my oath to my wife. I'll never get to her heaven now." Sten turned to look into the waves, staring far into the mass of water, endless and powerful. "I have broken the oath to her and her God. I left Ragnar all those years ago, and now I've also broken my oath to Ivar."

"Seems to me two of those oaths were worth breaking. The gods will see it that way." Sten had left Ivar's father, Ragnar Lothbrok's, service when he met his wife. Sten and Ragnar sailed the world together, forging a reputation as the greatest heroes of their age. "Do you miss her?"

Sten's head dropped, and he pulled at his long

silver beard. "Every day."

"If you had the chance again, would you do the same thing? Settle down with her, I mean?" Einar asked. Sten had done what Einar dreamed of. He had sacrificed his life at sea and war for the love of a woman. Sten had gone and lived a peaceful life on a Saxon hilltop and had done so for many years before she died. Then, Sten had lived peacefully with the Christ Monks before Einar had torn that peace into a bloody end.

"In a heartbeat," said Sten. "Living with my Ralla was the best time of my life. She was my everything. All else is just noise, Einar, just bluster and murder and blood."

Einar thought he heard the big man's voice crack, and Sten turned away to conceal whatever painful look those memories etched onto his hard face. But Sten's feelings were obvious, and they were more than simple words. Einar had a chance at that same happiness. If he could get through this war with Ivar, then he would do it. He would settle down with Hildr and enjoy the same peace that Sten had enjoyed with Ralla.

"You and Hildr are close?"

"We are," Einar admitted, knowing it would be much too obvious to hide his feelings.

"You should take the opportunity. Find some peace in the world. War and death and petty squabbles between rich men will go on without you."

"I think I will," Einar said quietly, almost as a whisper, as though it were something which should remain unspoken or unheard.

"So you'll go to Haesten in Wessex?"

"I won't. I don't think I will. Let's get through this fight first," said Einar, knowing his words were nonsense but reluctant to give firm voice to his dream.

"Hundr has sworn to go to Haesten when this is over."

"It's not my oath. I never swore. We said we would never serve another man again."

"I had no choice, old friend." It was Hundr's voice, and Einar glanced around to look at him, heat rising into his face, as it does when one is caught talking about a friend.

"When we sailed away, limping and bloody from Northumbria, we agreed we would be the masters of our own destiny. We would make our own way and not risk our lives at the whim of another Lord."

"I know what we agreed, but it was the only way. Ivar will never give up hunting us. Now he believes us dead, and we needed a ship from Haesten and some of his men to end this."

"And so you must fight for Haesten."

"I must. Kolo and Ragnhild will go with me, as will you Sten, I hope. Einar, you are free to do as you please, and I will help you go wherever you wish before I go to Haesten."

"I think I will try to find a place for Hildr and me."

"I want you to be happy, Einar. You took me in when I had nothing, and you attacked Hakon's fortress for me. I would do anything for you."

Einar placed a hand on Hundr's shoulder and searched his face. There was much pain there, not just the dark, angry scar running from forehead to jaw, or in the empty socket of his burned out eye, but in the remaining eye. Inside that deep pool of brown flecked with green, there was a lifetime of pain, an unfulfilled longing. Einar remembered the boy at the quayside, so full of hope and naivete. All that lad wanted was to be a warrior, and to make his reputation, just as Einar had at that age. It had only been a year and a half since that day, but Hundr looked ten years older. The unscarred half of his face was drawn and lined around his eye and down the hollow of his cheek.

"You are the leader here now. And after this," Einar waved his arm towards the shore. "I will try to find some happiness in what's left of my life. I hope you too can find happiness." *For the boy that you were, for that innocent face.*

"My happiness will come with Ivar's death."

I know, and I pity you for that.

The ship lurched beneath Einar's feet, and the three men grabbed rope or beam to steady themselves. The moment passed, and Hundr clapped Einar and Sten on the back and went to join Rollo, to talk of war again and how to lure the Boneless out into a trap.

"He has changed," said Sten, watching Hundr's back.

"He has. He's as fierce as any Viking Lord. Pitiless and cruel. Just as we once were," said Einar, recalling the moment they had slipped out of Frankia and Hundr repaid the oathbreakers for their treachery. Hundr had cut the throats of Guthmund and Hrorik. They had begged and wept, but Hundr had cut their throats and thrown their corpses over the side as easy as cutting a loaf of bread.

"Let's get the other ships, lads. We hunt today," Hundr called.

So this was it. They would draw the Boneless out, and surely one of Ivar or Hundr must die and end their hatred.

TWENTY FIVE

Hundr pulled hard, leaning back and allowing the muscles across his shoulders to bunch as he hauled back on the oar. Reaching to full stretch, he twisted his wrist, and the smooth oar shaft left the water, and all resistance disappeared. He breathed out and leant forward, bringing the oar blade back again for another long stroke.

"Pull," said Rollo at the bow, keeping the ship on target.

Hundr looked across the bench where Kolo pulled in unison with him, but on the opposite side of the ship, his huge muscles glistening with sweat and rippling under his skin. Only six of them rowed this captured drakkar warship, and another six rowed the remaining two of Ivar's ships taken in the recent fighting. Hundr grunted and heaved again in time with Rollo's orders. Kolo grinned at him as he hauled on his oar. Hundr wondered if his friend secretly felt the same pang of fear as he did for the slaughter which must surely come this day. They rowed north now, out of the gift of the wind and away from the small island where he had hidden the three captured ships. Soon, when Rollo caught sight of Dublin's port, they would bank west and into the wind, then the sails could be raised, and the back-breaking rowing work would be over. But that was when the gamble of that day's fighting would begin, when the pieces of Hundr's plan would fall into place, or not. To the south of Ivar's base at Dublin lay a collection of four small islands. One of which was large and inhabited by Christ Priests, but the other three were uninhabited and had provided a safe haven for Hundr and his warriors to wait in safety for the right time to attack.

Dublin itself was a large and prosperous port set at the juncture where the long, wide river Liffey met the Irish Sea. Ivar had been ruler of Dublin, and therefore most of the East Coast of Ireland, for almost ten years. From his time with Ivar, Sten had seen the wealth flowing into Ivar's chests. That wealth came from the markets within the town and from the fruitful farmlands spreading westwards along the river's slow winding journey inland. The town of Dublin lay on a corner of land cut from the south bank of the Liffey. That spit of land wound around from the river and into a secure port built around a deep black pool, which gave Dublin its Irish name, Dubh Linn. To get to that port, one must sail through a narrow spit of water and along Dublin's fortified walls before entering the black pool and its busy wharves. The town looked down onto its port from a gravelly hill, and its location made Dublin both easily defensible and gave it a commanding view of the Liffey, the sea to the east, and the lands to the southwest.

Hundr pulled again, his back screaming from the effort of hauling the warship northwards. Six men were barely a third of a crew, and the going was slow and muscle burning. He had been through the layout of Dublin with Sten over and again, each night for the last week, trying to build a picture in his mind. He, Einar, Sten, Ragn-hild, and Rollo had debated the town and where its weak points might be, but Hundr knew there could be no assault on the town. It was high-walled and heavily manned by Ivar's Northmen and his Irish warriors. To access the town, they would need to sail into the black pool. Any ship taking that channel must pass by Dublin's long, high walls and through the narrow waterway, all the time under the watch, and missile fire, of the city's warriors before making landfall. Then, any attacking force would need to climb a steep gravel-strewn hill into another hail of missiles. So, to kill Ivar, Hundr knew he had to flush the Boneless out of his lair and fight outside of the

town. Hundr had to hope that Ivar was suffi-
ciently furious at the loss of his three ships and
crews to be taunted out of his stronghold. If he
ventured out on to the water to fight the men
who had affronted him, then it would be a brutal
fight at sea. It would be a clash of arms across
the bows where any mailed or armoured warrior
who fell overboard would sink to a terrible choking death in the deep dark waters where the river
turned to sea if a blade didn't kill that warrior
first.

Hundr had soaked up all Sten could tell him
about Dublin and about the safety and security
of the wharves inside the curve of the black pool.
The gut-gnawing worry on that bright, late summer morning as he sailed up the Irish Sea was
that Ivar had more ships tucked away in that un-
assailable port. Hundr, Sten, Einar, and Ragnhild
had all agreed that Ivar had five ships remaining, three of which patrolled the river and two
within the port itself. They had watched, and the
painted bows and differing beast heads marked
out those ships, making it a simple matter to tell
the difference. What worried Hundr was if those
three were not his only ships patrolling the river
and surrounding sea. If Ivar's son had more, even
fat-bellied knar trading ships, hidden behind the
black pool. That would mean death and pain for
Hundr and his crew. Ivar and his son would have
hundreds of warriors within Dublin's walls, war-

riors from Denmark and Norway, spear Danes and Norsemen, along with the famously wild and ferocious Irish warriors. It would be a simple thing to load up those hidden vessels with warriors and launch out into the Liffey's span to trap and slaughter Hundr and his crew. Which was why he hauled now on the back-breaking oar and why only six of them heaved the ship into view of where the Liffey chopped into the Irish coastline.

Sweat trickled down Hundr's spine beneath his jerkin, laying light on his back. He wore no mail and no weapons as he rowed, and nor did the other five rowers nor the rowers in the two other of Ivar's captured ships. It was a gift from the gods not to be wearing his mail when heaving the warship against the tide, but Hundr felt exposed. He felt unprotected. Should they be boarded now by Ivar's warriors, it would be simple butcher work for them, like cutting down livestock. Being boarded and killed was not, however, the worst thing that could happen to Hundr that day. To sail into Ivar's maw unarmoured and hugely outnumbered like this, Hundr risked being captured, being taken alive, and delivered into Ivar's hands. Again, the image of the blood-eagled King Aelle flashed before Hundr's eyes, the unspeakable pain the King endured when his ribs were chipped slowly away from his spine.

"Ten more strokes, lads. Ten big ones and then we'll get her up," said Rollo, and the rowers all shouted in glee. Hundr pulled, and Kolo smiled at him again. Hundr grinned back this time. The plan was underway now. Soon it would be too late to turn back. Once they were in the river, the city would know their presence and eyes would be upon them. So Hundr smiled, and pushed the fear out of his belly, replacing it with the memory of his hate for Ivar. Hate for the man whose son had taken his eye, hate for the man who had taken the love of Hundr's life, and hate for the man who would pursue him to the ends of the earth. At the tenth stroke, the six rowers all leaned on their oar shafts, gasping for breath and pouring with sweat.

"Right, lads. Stow them, and let's get her hoisted," said Rollo. Hundr pulled his oar in over the side and secured it in its hemp loops. Then he joined Kolo to haul on the sealskin ropes, and the sail slowly came up. The long, sleek ship came about, and the sail snapped full, catching hold of the westerly wind blowing towards Ireland's green hills.

"Well done, Rollo," Hundr said, for they were on course. Sailing straight for the wide mouth of the river, and alongside them were Ivar's two other captured ships.

"So far, so good," said Rollo. His eyes met Hundr's, and they were ablaze, his scarred face flashing a gap-toothed smile at the thought of the fight to come.

"We can't jump too early. We must get close enough to close up the pool," Hundr said, and the six nodded their understanding. For that was the reason they sailed the captured ships with the lowest possible number of oarsmen. They would steer those ships into the broad river Liffey, and then once sure that the three captured ships were steered toward the black pool, Hundr the other crew would jump overboard and wait there in the cold river water for the Wave Bear to pick them up and haul them on board, where their arms and armour awaited. Hundr knew that if he could clog up the thin slip of river water between the Liffey and the black pool where the town of Dublin curved around, then there could be no surprises. Even if Ivar had ten warships and men to crew them in that safe port, they could not get out. All Ivar would have would be his three warships already in the river and anchored safely there. Hundr sighed and clenched his teeth. Even if that part of the plan worked and Ivar came out to fight, he would still have three crews. Three crews against Hundr's one.

The ship picked up pace now that the wind filled the sail, and Kolo leant on the tiller, guiding her straight towards the river's mouth.

"I forgot to tell you something, my friend," Kolo said above the creaking of the ship's ropes and the rush of the waves crashing against the hull.

"What?"

"I can't swim," said the huge African warrior, and then bellowed with laughter, throwing his head back into the wind. Rollo and the other men laughed along. *I hope you are joking.*

Hundr looked back, and the Wave Bear was there in the distance. She couldn't get too close, not yet, because there would be danger in those moments when they sent the captured ships on their trajectory into the black pool, but the distance between them was a risk. Hundr and the others would be in the water, and should Ivar's men get onto their ships quickly, then Hundr would be stuck in the water like a piece of driftwood. All Ivar's men would need to do is row twenty or thirty strokes and skewer him where he flailed in the water, or grab him up out of the Sea God Njorth's watery embrace and take him to Ivar where torture, unspeakable pain, and death awaited. Hundr swallowed the lump of fear down from his throat. All six men around him knew the risk. They coasted along under the speed of the wind, into the jaws of death. Hundr had told them that even if the plan worked, and Ivar came out to fight, the odds were still against them, but they did it anyway. Three captured ships sailed up the Liffey and into Ivar's maw, and Hundr's warriors loved the thrill of it, the anticipation of the fight to come, the chance to feel battle joy, that fleeting sensation that lifts a man beyond the mundane grimness of everyday life and up into the heightened sense of glory and skill.

"Keep an eye now," Hundr warned them, "Watch for Ivar's ships."

They sailed into Dublin's bay, and to the north, the long line of Bull Island was a hazy, shimmering break in the grey horizon as they raced across the bay and on into the river's mouth. Hundr could see men on Dublin's walls. Men whose shining spear points matched the grey sky above and the deep iron grey of the water beneath the ship's hull. He knew those men would sound the warning as they saw three warships approaching at speed from the south. But it would be too late, and Hundr allowed himself a grin. It was too late because he was bringing war to Ivar the Boneless. *Let him feel what it's like to be hunted. I don't run anymore. I am drengr, and I am the hunter.*

"Get the fire going," he said to Rollo. He nodded, and they both moved the pile of timber and moss peat they had collected in the bilge at the mast's base. Rollo lifted a smoking faggot and blew on its end. He cozened it and touched it at the carefully shielded kindling. He blew on it again, and Hundr saw the orange glow, flickering at first, dancing precariously in the wind. But then it crackled and sprang into life, the sea air giving it life as it spread across the kindling and on slowly onto the hill of timber they had prepared. Rollo handled the flaming faggot branch and handed it to Hundr, and he went to the port side and waved it in a wide arc, first one way and then other. For that was the signal, the sign he had told the other ships to watch for. They would also set their fires to blaze. He could feel the heat from the fire in the bilge, and the six men moved towards the steerboard to join Kolo. Hundr saw warriors gathered on the city walls, warriors pointing and shouting in their direction. *Ivar will know now. They will have told him some daring warrior has come to attack him in his lair, to challenge the great champion. I hope he feels a pang of fear, and I hope he fears it's me.*

"Guide her in now, tie off the rudder," said Rollo, and Kolo brought her around and towards the channel leading into the black pool. Hundr could see the gravel hill running down to the water's edge on the town side of the river. The wind gusted into the sail, and the ship jerked to port. The beast head prow was suddenly no longer aiming for the channel but for the town walls.

"Bring her back, Kolo, now!" Hundr shouted. Kolo pulled the rudder back towards him. They were getting too close now, and the fire had caught the woollen sailcloth, licking up its edges like a hungry dragon's tongue. The heat blew hard against his face, and Hundr held his hand up to shield his one good eye from the furnace.

"We go too far. We must jump now," roared Rollo above the din of the fire. Hundr leant over the side and saw the other two crews had already jumped, their ships under sail and flaming, heading into the channel. He could see the warriors' heads bobbing in the water like paddling ducks.

"She's on track. Tie her off," Hundr said, watching the beast head prow come about and point at the channel and on into the black pool. Kolo tied a rope around the tiller and secured it to the sternpost.

"Jump!" bellowed Rollo, and the others leapt overboard. Hundr waited for two more heartbeats to make sure the ship was on course and then put his hand on the smooth wood of the ship's side and launched himself over the side. The river water crashed up around his chest and ears, the cold sucking his breath away and cooling his face where the fire had warmed it. He trod water, his legs kicking like frogs' legs, and he turned, flailing with his arms to see if the ships had made it. Hundr clenched his jaw and nodded as he watched their trajectory. All three ships pushed on into the wide black pool, the middle vessel canting over to one side as her mast cracked and fell under the blaze at the base of her hull. Three fire ships blocked the channel, trapping Ivar's two remaining warships and any other vessels he might bring to bear in the battle to come. *Surely that's enough now to bring you out, you bastard. I'm here for you. I've taken three of your ships and sent them burning into your city.*

Hundr swam to where Kolo and Rollo waited in the choppy river water.

"They went in. There'll be mayhem in there now," said Rollo, his chin barely above the water-line. "This water is bloody freezing. My balls are shrinking into my body."

"There she is," said Kolo, pointing downriver where the Wave Bear's sail and prow were coming towards them, but still distant. They would be in the river water for a while yet. Hundr looked across at the other two groups of bobbing heads in the wide river.

"Swim to the closest group there," said Hundr. Otherwise, the Wave Bear would have to drop sail and row to each group, an awkward manoeuvre which would take time. And surely Ivar must come soon. Hundr swam, the cold salty water lapping at his face and his legs heavy. He could see Bush waving at him and he kicked towards him.

"It's bloody freezing," said Bush, his teeth chattering. Hundr came to rest alongside him with Kolo, Rollo, and the others close behind him. Thirteen men now treaded water together in the wide space between the Liffey and Irish Sea. The other group of six were some ways away and had drifted with the current towards the city and past the channel which led into the black pool.

"Mayhem in there now," said Bush, nodding towards the channel. "Shame to see such fine ships burn, though."

"Hopefully it makes him mad enough."

"He'll be mad alright. He is at the best of times. When Ivar hears some crazed bastard sent three fire ships into his port, he'll be madder than a kicked badger."

"Ship, ship!" one man behind Bush yelped, pointing frantically upriver. Hundr pulled at the water with his arm and twisted his torso to look where the warrior pointed. He cursed under his breath, for one of Ivar's ships was already in the river. Only two must rest at port further downstream, and this one was already out on patrol and heading straight for them. Hundr craned his neck to see where the Wave Bear was, and she was closing but still too distant.

"She won't make it," said Kolo. He was right. Ivar's warship was already too close. Her crew was pounding their oars, and she looked big.

"Is it the Windspear?" asked Rollo, which was Ivar's huge warship, and one of the ships he had brought to Frankia to pursue Hundr.

"Not big enough," said a warrior, and Hundr thought he was right. Windspear was longer and wider in the hull. He blew out his cheeks in relief. If it had been the Windspear, it would have Ivar on board. It was too soon for Ivar to join the fight. Hundr needed to be on board the Wave

Bear when Ivar brought his savagery onto the river, not floating helplessly in the river where Ivar could simply fish him out like a floundering seal.

"Swim, lads, swim!" Bush yelled downriver towards the isolated in the water.

"Swim towards the Wave Bear, now," said Hundr, and he took off pumping his arms into the water. He knew the ship wasn't close enough. Ivar's ship would be upon them before they reached her. The third crew of six were lost, good men and brave, but Ivar's ship had reached them. Six of Hundr's men would die in the icy river, with no blades in hand, and as Hundr listened to their shouts and cries on the wind, the price for his battle with Ivar felt heavy. *This is the price of reputation, of being a leader.* It was the cold-hearted, brutal decision-making that Hundr had lacked in Northumbria, and when the Seaworm had sailed aimlessly up and down the Frankish coast, wondering what to do next and where to go. This was what to do next, kill his enemies and do that which must be done without hesitation.

"They have them," shouted Rollo. Hundr's ears were like ice, so cold in the water that they hurt. He didn't look back, but he could hear them dying. Ahead, the Wave Bear came closer. He could see the faces of her crew now. He could see Ragnhild leaning over the side and pointing towards him. The third crew were dying in the cold river, but Hundr would make it to the Wave Bear before Ivar's ship caught them.

"Two more ships coming," came a shout. Hundr's stomach plummeted, for Ivar had surely boarded his ship. The Windspear was being launched, and Ivar would cram her with fierce warriors, warriors with sword and axe, skilled men who came to kill Hundr and his crew. Ivar would be shouting and cursing and urging his men on to fight and kill. He would be baying for blood and bringing his big, bearded killers to this desperate fight on the Liffey. Hundr twisted again in the water. He saw Ivar's warriors crowding to hang over the side of their warship to hack and stab at Hundr's lost men. They flailed their arms and screamed in terror as spear points turned the grey-green water red with their blood, and their corpses sank into Njorth's depths and away from the world and from Valhalla.

TWENTY SIX

Ragnhild grabbed his wrist and hauled him up. Hundr kicked his legs to gain purchase on the hull, and then Einar's flat face appeared over the side. Einar reached down and grabbed a meaty fistful of Hundr's jerkin and hauled him up. He crashed to the deck, coughing and spluttering, freezing saltwater stinging his dead eye.

"The first ship is underway again. We must move quickly," said Ragnhild, kneeling to look him in the eye. Hundr nodded and wiped the water from his face.

"To oars, get ready," Hundr shouted, fighting against the crippling cramp of the freezing water in his muscles. He clenched his jaw to stop his teeth from chattering and forced himself to his feet. The deck of the Sea Bear was alive with warriors pulling on mail and readying blades. Others sat back at benches from where they had hauled the desperate men of Hundr's crew out of the water.

"There's still a chance to get out of this," said Ragnhild, grabbing him by the shoulder, "We can bring her about and be out to sea before they catch us."

"No more running, Ragnhild. We kill Ivar today, or we die trying."

She nodded and drew her axe. "To war then."

"Row, you lazy whores, put your backs into it," bellowed Sten, stalking the deck. His huge double-bladed axe, Warbringer, resting on his broad shoulder. The ship lurched forward, and the rowers grunted. Einar came forth with Hundr's mail and helped him shrug it on over his head and strap his sword belt on. Hundr would wear Soulstealer at his waist and Munin at his back, but in this fight, there would be no room for swords. It would be close work, face-to-face murder work. So he took an axe from Einar in his right hand and a dagger in his left. Hundr jumped up onto the mast platform where the men could see him.

"Today, we fight Ivar the Boneless, Champion of the North, son of Ragnar Lothbrok. He out-numbers us, and he has three ships. We have one, but we are all champions here. If we do this today, our reputations will sing across the years, and when grandfathers tell children stories at firesides, they will speak our names and of

317

our deeds. We attack the Boneless in his home, in his own fortress. We are the wolves and bears of the sea. We are the greatest warriors in all the world," he shouted and held his axe aloft. The warriors cheered and roared at his words because what he said was true. They attacked now to make their legend and earn their places beside the heroes of Valhalla. "Remember, do it as we practiced. Ready shields and charge them. Don't fight them. Just get them overboard. We need to kill them as quickly as we can before the other two ships arrive."

They had spent the last few days practising the drill. Hundr had them form pairs of overlapped shields and charge the decks. At first, it had been an awkward mess. A ship's deck was no place for a shield charge, but eventually, the crew had found their own spaces, and they had been over it repeatedly until they were ready.

"Get the hooks ready," ordered Sten. The warriors dragged out the long hooks Hundr had designed days earlier. They were simply oars from Ivar's captured ships with carved hooks fixed to their ends. "Here they come. Brace yourselves."

Hundr kept the crook of his arm around the mast pole, and beyond the snarling bear of the ship's prow, he could see the bearded faces on the charging ship. They sped towards the Wave Bear, and Hundr watched their dropping oar blades rise in unison and fold inwards like giant wings to be stowed safely. At the last minute, her steersmen would veer to port and bring her hull alongside the Wave Bear, and they would pour spears and arrows onto her deck before attempting to board her and subdue the crew.

The enemy ship came on, and Hundr could see the snarling dragon at her prow, and then he felt the thud as the two ships came together in a crunch of timber which threw him forwards. Hundr clattered into the bilge, banging his ribs and elbow on a rowing bench and coming up snarling.

"Shields, shields," Sten roared. The crew followed the drill and braced two long steps away from where the enemy ship came alongside. Sure enough, grimacing bearded faces came into view and hurled spears onto the deck of the Wave Bear, but Hundr's crew crouched behind shields, and the enemy injured no one in that first exchange of blows.

"Archers," Hundr shouted, and Ragnhild, Hildr, and three other crewmen leapt up onto rowing benches and began to loose their arrows across the bows. Hundr nodded with satisfaction as an enemy reeled away, clutching with bloody fingers at an arrow sunk into his cheek.

"Wait," Hundr ordered. He crouched behind the wall of ten shield men, and he sensed them edging forward with anticipation. But timing was everything, and it had to be perfect. Hundr had to get this first crew of Ivar's men out of the way before the other two crews arrived; otherwise the Wave Bear would be overwhelmed with Ivar's warriors, and that would mean certain death. The ship came to a stop beneath his feet as the two warships came fully alongside each other. He watched the enemy closely, waiting for the right time to strike. He saw boots appear on the edge of the enemy bows and heard their commander shouting.

"Go, go, go," shouted their leader.

That was the sign he had been waiting for. "Now," he shouted, and the line of shield men grunted in unison and took two big steps forward. Ten shields came to bear just as Ivar's warriors made the leap across the slim space between the two ships, but as they jumped, the force of their leaps pushed the ships apart a forearm's width further, and Hundr's shield men simply barged and banged those daring warriors backwards. They shrieked and shouted, wide-eyed and grasping for handholds before disappearing into the cold water between the ships, dragged down to the depths by their mail or heavy leather breastplates. Hundr nodded with grim satisfaction. *It's working.*

"Back," he said, and the shield men took two steps back. Another line of attackers leapt over the gap as the two ships came together again.

"In pairs, attack," Hundr said, and the shield men pushed forward in pairs, barging the fresh attackers overboard. But Ivar's men were fighting back now and holding against the press of shields against them. Ragnhild and the archers were picking off men with their bows, and Hundr, Kolo, and Sten struck in between the line of shields with the axes. All was chaos and blood, shouting and carnage.

A small, bull-necked warrior roared orders at his warriors from the deck of the enemy ship, and his men stopped leaping across the bows onto the Wave Bear, they had lost a third of their crew already to Hundr's organised defence, and their leader ordered his men to form up. He had them raise their own shields so that two shield walls faced off across the ships, and his warriors heaved the two bows together and pulled the ships touching tight, removing the sea gap between them. Hundr leapt backwards and ran to the stern, and his breath caught in his chest as he saw Ivar's two remaining ships across the bay. They were now fully underway and were rowing at speed in their direction. Killing this first crew was taking too long, and the bull-necked captain had turned the fight from a failing assault into a shield wall battle at sea. Hundr knew the captain hoped he could hold the Wave Bear long enough for Ivar to join the fray and overwhelm the Wave Bear with sheer numbers as he boarded her from the other side.

Hundr cursed, and he braced himself. He had to turn the tide of the fight again. If he didn't get rid of this first enemy crew, then it was all over. Ivar would descend on them and turn the river Liffey red with their blood.

"Ragnhild," he shouted to the Valkyrie, and she looked at him from where she still stood high on a rowing bench, firing arrows. "Fire on the first rank. Keep their shields up."

She nodded, her battle experience allowing her to understand immediately what he planned to do. He had to break their shield wall, and if she could keep their shields high, he knew he could do it. Ragnhild and Hildr poured a steady stream of shafts into that front enemy rank. An arrow tonked off a tall warrior's helmet, and another roared in pain as one sunk into a warrior's neck between his baked leather breastplate and his head.

"Sten," Hundr called, looking for his old friend. The old warrior was behind the front line, waiting for the shield walls to come together so he could strike over the line of linden wood with his enormous axe. "On me," Hundr said, and the old man nodded.

Hundr took a deep breath and gripped his axe and knife tightly in each hand. Then he sped forward. In three steps, he was behind his own shield wall, and they moved apart to allow him through. Hundr crouched and slashed his axe blade across the thighs of two warriors in the enemy shield wall line. Those two men lowered their shields, and one man fell with one of Ragnhild's arrows in his eye, and Hundr rose to cut the throat of the second man with his knife. Hot blood spurted from the dying man's throat, and Hundr shoved him backwards and raised his foot onto the side of the enemy ship. He gasped as he felt a monstrous shove in his back, and they propelled him forwards and through the opposing shield wall to land sprawling on the deck of the enemy ship. Hundr turned, raising his weapons to protect himself from the enemy blades, which must surely come for him, and blood rushed into his ears as panic swarmed him. But no enemy attacked him, Sten had thrown Hundr through the hole he had made in the enemy shield wall and then charged into it himself and now lay about him with Warbringer, whose twin blades were thick with gore and men shrank back from the horror of the huge death-dealing warrior.

Hundr scrambled to his feet and darted towards the bull-necked captain, who pushed and shoved at his men to reform their line. But it was too late. Kolo and Rollo had boarded the enemy ship behind Sten, and now more Wave Bear men followed, and the enemy ship was in rout. Bull Neck sensed Hundr's approach and turned just in time to see the axe blade coming for his face, the captain squeezed his eyes closed, flinching from the shining arc coming for him. Hundr grunted as the axe slapped into the captain's forehead, the blow jarring his arm as it split Bull Necks skull. He fell mewing to the deck as his lifeblood poured down his face, and Hundr watched with satisfaction as the rest of the enemy crew were put to the sword or thrown over the side.

Across the choppy waters, Ivar's remaining two ships closed in. It would be a matter of heart-beats until they were upon them. Hundr closed his eyes and controlled his racing heart. *This is it. He is here. One of us must die today.* Hundr ordered his men back onto the Wave Bear, and they used their long hooks to keep the defeated enemy ship close so that Ivar must either sail in difficulty around the other side to board the Wave Bear under a barrage of arrows or attack across the deck of the first lost ship. Sten turned to Hundr, his grey beard flecked with blood and his eyes wild with battle fury.

"He's coming, lad. Let's get it done once and for all."

Hundr nodded his agreement and leapt back onto the Wave Bear's deck. They had lost two men, and another four were wounded but still able to fight. Ragnhild and Hildr scampered around the enemy ship, looking for arrows to re-use. The warriors checked shield straps and drank from ale skins, preparing themselves for the onslaught, for this would be the proper test. So far, Hundr's plan had worked. He had sealed the black pool and stopped two of Ivar's warships and any unseen docked ships from entering the battle, limiting Ivar to his three river-borne ships. One of those ships' crews was already dead, but now Ivar came with two full crews of warriors, which could be close to a hundred men.

"Remember, we don't have to kill them all. Once we kill Ivar, it's over. The fight will go out of them."

"It's no simple thing to kill the son of Ragnar and Champion of the North," grumbled one red-haired warrior whose shield lay broken in three places from the previous fight.

"Leave him to me. Just do as we practiced. It already worked once. We do the same thing again," said Hundr. For that was his plan. Keep the shield wall tight and let Ivar come on. His higher numbers didn't matter because the ship created a narrow battlefield where the only way Ivar could overlap Hundr's line was to bring one of his ships around to the rear. Hundr hoped Ivar would be too furious to think of that. He hoped Ivar's rage would cloud his judgement. Ivar had seen his port burned and his men killed. He would want blood.

"Better make sure Ivar knows who he's fighting." Hundr jumped back onto the enemy ship and went to stand high on the steerboard. He drew Soulstealer and Munin from their scabbards and held them out wide. The two ships' oar blades rose and fell in perfect time, sending glittering water droplets shimmering into the sea air. Hundr could see snarling faces over the sides of both vessels, and there it was. Ivar's green cape flapped in the wind, and Hundr saw him there in the prow, sword in hand and urging his men to row faster. Hundr couldn't make out his features, and he couldn't see what damage his axe throw had wrought on Ivar's handsome face, but he knew the Boneless saw him. He would be unmistakable with his two swords and his one eye. That thought caused Hundr to pause. The battle lust fled from him like water pouring from a jug. He sensed she was close, Saoirse, his one love. His lost Irish Princess. She was there watching somewhere on the walls.

He searched those long battlements, but they were too far away to recognise any of the hundreds of heads watching the sea battle unfold before them. Hundr just knew she was there, pregnant with Ivar's child. He wondered if she ever thought of him, as he thought of her every day. Sadness swelled in his chest, and Hundr let his swords fall to his sides. Even if he killed Ivar and ended their mutual hatred, she would still not come to him. She would still need to stay here and keep the peace between her people and the occupying Viking invaders. In the end, he knew that whilst Ivar hated him for killing his son and beating him in single combat, he hated Ivar because he had everything Hundr did not. Ivar had Saoirse, her dazzling beauty and humour were his, and Hundr would never feel the warmth of her company again. Ivar had wealth, power, and reputation, and Hundr had nothing. He sheathed his swords and picked up his axe and knife. He might have nothing now but kill Ivar, and he would be the most famous Viking warrior in all Midgard, in all the world. His name would be on men's lips from Norway to Novgorod. He would fulfil his oath and go to Haesten in Wessex, but then he would become his own man, a Jarl and a warlord, to rival the legend of Ragnar Lothbrok. Hundr set his jaw and beckoned to Ivar with his axe. The anger and fury welled within him again.

"Here they come," said Kolo, planting himself in the shield wall.

"Death to Ivar the Boneless, or we drink together this night in Valhalla," shouted Hundr, and the crew cheered. From the corner of his eye, Hundr saw Einar standing behind the battle line. His axe still at his belt, and his face ashen white. Hundr went to him and placed a hand on his shoulder.

"What is it?" he said. Einar looked him in the eye, and Einar's own eyes quivered in their

327

sockets. He licked at dry lips.

"It's gone from me, the battle fury. Ivar took it with his blade. I can't…"

"You are Einar Rosti, Einar the Brawler, and you are a killer. I need you now Einar. If you want to live and have your future with Hildr, you need to fight. You need to draw your axe and kill our enemies with your old ferocity." Hundr clapped him on the shoulder and leant to grab a rowing bench as he lost his balance. Ivar's ship had slammed into the empty vessel, and his warriors roared their battle cries and poured from their ship onto the deck of the already conquered boat.

"Shield wall," Sten bellowed, and the shields came together with a crack and the grunt of men readying themselves for battle, for the blood and blades to come. One of Ivar's warriors ran across the deck, his face bright red and eyes wide behind a bushy black beard. He brandished a short sword and flew towards the Wave Bear as though he had lost his mind with anger. But that blood-crazed warrior stopped in his tracks as an arrow from Hildr's bow slammed into his groin, and he looked down and grabbed at the shaft, looking up again in horror as Sten's axe took his head with a wet slap. Blood pumped from the headless man's torso, adding to the coating of filth from the earlier exchange, and a second man lost his footing and leapt backwards away from Warbringer's wide swing.

"Come and die, bastards," Sten growled and pulled back beyond the shield wall.

"This is a rare fight, my friends," grinned Kolo, and he braced his shield, laughing with joy at the danger of it all.

Ivar's men came to a stop, breathing hard. The grim-faced men parted, and Ivar shouldered his way through his warriors to the edge of the ship's deck. He searched the line and pointed his sword at Hundr.

"You dare attack me here," he growled, visibly shaking. His was blade quivering in his hand. "I want that one alive, kill the others, but that one is mine."

"That looks sore," said Hundr and pointed his axe at Ivar's face. A red and purple gash stretched across Ivar's cheek and into his hairline. The scar from the axe Hundr had thrown at him in Frankia. Ivar just spat in his direction. "Did you think I was dead, you fool? Are you going to fight, or have you come to bargain, to make a back-handed deal like you did in Frankia. We come to fight, and to kill you, Ivar."

Ivar lowered his blade, and his men roared, launching themselves across to the deck of the Wave Bear.

"Now, now!" shouted Hundr. He had allocated six men to this, the irrevocable part of his plan.

He watched them, fear gnawing away at his insides, but it worked, and they shoved the enemy ship away with the long hooks, away just enough to make an arm's length gap between the boats. His men did as they had done before and threw Ivar's warriors back with their shields and into the icy grip of the river water. Six of Ivar's men fell into the water, and they made no sound as their heavy clothing and arms dragged them down. Another line came on, and Hundr's men did the same. Another four men fell into the Liffey, but two held on, clinging to shield rims, but Kolo and Rollo stabbed and kicked those men over the side with ease.

Ivar ordered his men back, and he nodded a stony stare at Hundr, his odd coloured eyes glinting beneath knitted brows. He had lost twelve men already, but a smile grew across his handsome face as his second ship came about the Wave Bear and behind Hundr's shield wall line. Hundr saw the worst had happened. Ivar had surrounded them.

TWENTY SEVEN

Ivar's second ship came about the Wave Bear in a wide turn, and Hundr saw her brimming with Irish warriors, unmistakable in their brightly coloured plaid cloaks. Her oars rose and fell, bringing the ship around. It would only be a few heartbeats before she came alongside.

"Second shield wall on me. Ragnhild, Hildr, Einar, on me," Hundr called.

He grabbed a shield and made himself ready. He had to trust that Sten, Kolo, and Rollo would hold the other side of the ship against Ivar and his warriors. The second ship grew closer, and Hundr saw the great bushy head of Cormac, the leader of Ivar's wild Irish warriors. Hundr had met him at a feast during the war in Northumbria, and they had drunk and laughed together that night as friends. But now, that big Irishman came to kill Hundr with sharp blades and fierce warriors. Einar banged his shield next

to Hundr's, and Hildr took her place next to
Einar. Ragnhild joined her shield, and their wall
was ready. Hundr looked at their faces, drawn
and sweating from the fight, and his heart
swelled.

"If I am to die here on this river, I am glad it
is with you," he said and looked each of them in
the eye. Behind him, Hundr heard the roar and
clash of weapons on timber as the fight started
with Ivar's crew. He wanted to turn and see what
happened there, to see if the Boneless had broken
through and even at that moment made ready
to chop a blade into his back, but he couldn't
look, because the second ship crunched alongside the Wave Bear, and they all sagged to their
right, losing balance under the impact. A scream
came from Hundr's left, but it was his blind side,
his dead eye side, and so he couldn't see. A roar
followed that scream, a gut-wrenching animal
sound, deafening and terrible, like some monstrous beast howling in the wilderness. The roar
came again, and Hundr saw a shield fly across the
side to clatter into the Irishmen, and then Hundr
staggered as he saw Einar jump the distance between the ships. Einar made the jump with axe in
hand and clattered into the bunched Irishmen,
reckless of their blades and knocking most of
them backwards. Einar stood and roared again,
this time swinging his axe across a man's throat,
spraying thick crimson across the deck. Then

he was moving, fast and deadly, amongst them. Einar cut and slashed, and the Irishmen, famed for their wild ferocity, crept back away from his war madness.

Hundr twisted to see what had caused Einar's rage and saw Hildr crouched with a bloody wound in her thigh, and Ragnhild held her shield aloft to protect her Valkyrie sister. Hundr laughed. Amidst the death and screaming he laughed, because Einar Rosti had found his fury and was cutting a swathe of death amongst Cormac's warriors. Hundr leapt to join Einar, and an Irishman jabbed a spear at his face, and Hundr dodged that blow and stabbed his knife into his attacker's belly. He felt a blow glance from his shoulder and turned to see Cormac coming for him with a bright sword. The Irishman lunged for Hundr's belly, and Hundr threw himself onto the deck to avoid the blow. He rolled and came up to duck another sweep of Cormac's blade. Then the Irishman's face went still, and he dropped his sword. Cormac pitched over, face first at Hundr's feet, with Einar's axe buried in the back of his skull.

Ragnhild, Hildr, and Sten, along with five of the Wave Bear's crew, were also onboard Ivar's second ship. Two of those warriors had fallen to Irish blades, but the Irish had lost ten men dead or wounded to Hundr and Einar's attack. Einar was still driving them back, and Ragnhild ducked and weaved amongst their blades like a demon, cutting at their faces and chests, screaming for Odin to watch her deeds. The Irishmen threw down their weapons, and Einar opened the belly of a surrendered warrior, spilling stinking blue coils onto the blood-slick deck.

"Enough," Hundr called. "Over the side if you want to live." The Irishmen looked at each other and quickly decided it was better to take their chances in the river than face Einar's fury again. And so the survivors of Cormac's crew leapt overboard, even though the weight of their war gear would likely drag them to the depths. Hundr clenched his teeth and wiped the blood from his face.

Onboard the Wave Bear, Ivar had driven a wedge through the shield wall, and he fought there himself between the lines. Half of Hundr's men were dead, and he saw Kolo had taken a wound to his shoulder and was staggering beneath Ivar's whirring blade. Kolo parried one blow, but Ivar kicked the big man backwards, and Kolo rolled away, scrambling for his life. Hundr leapt back onboard the Wave Bear, following Sten, who made the same jump.

"We are still outnumbered," he said over Sten's shoulder, as the old man held firm beneath the axe and sword blades beating on his shield.

"Kill Ivar then, kill the bastard," Sten said.

Hundr tried to steady himself, watching Ivar cut down another of Rollo's men. Then Rollo himself came to face Ivar. Haesten's man chopped his axe into the enemy closest to Ivar and then confronted the Boneless. Ivar cut at Rollo, and Rollo parried the blow, but Ivar head-butted him hard in the face and brought his knee behind Rollo's leg, toppling him to the deck. Ivar fell upon Rollo's chest and sawed his blade back and forth across Rollo's throat, and Haesten's brave warrior died beneath Ivar's wrath.

Hundr tried to push himself forward, to face his great enemy, but something rooted his feet to the spot. He had watched Ivar kill his friend, but Rollo's death didn't spur Hundr on. His stomach clenched, and his throat became parched. Ivar's warriors had Rollo's surviving men pinned back at the opposite end of the Wave Bear, and there could be only three or four of them left fighting. On Hundr's end, there was only Sten, two of Rollo's warriors, and now Einar had joined them to beat back Ivar's men. A bald Norseman died beneath Sten's axe, and there was a gap, a clear opening between Hundr and Ivar. He forced himself forwards and shouted a challenge, barging past Sten and into the open space between the two fighting lines. Ivar turned to meet him, his sword swinging like a blur, and Hundr only just parried it with his knife, but Ivar twisted his blade, and the knife flew from Hundr's hand.

The Boneless snarled and came again, cutting and lunging faster than Hundr believed possible. Ivar's sword cut Hundr across the forehead and slashed a gash across his left forearm. He fell back beneath Ivar's rage, the Champion of the North screaming incoherently as he used all his speed and skill to beat Hundr back. He couldn't get a strike in. Ivar was just too fast. Hundr realised that the surrounding fighting had stopped, and the warriors on both sides watched the clash of leaders. Ivar made to strike again, but his foot slipped in a pool of gore and he fell to one knee. Hundr cut with his axe and it banged into Ivar's left hand, cutting two fingers away and sending one of his swords flying into the water. Ivar bellowed, and blood spurted from his fingers. He grabbed Hundr's face with that ruined hand, and hot blood washed across Hundr's mouth and into his throat. He retched and coughed but couldn't shake off his enemy. Hundr dropped his axe and clawed at Ivar's face, feeling the wet of Ivar's eye and twisting his nails as deep as he could. Ivar fell back, and Hundr leapt upon him, punching and head-butting and shouting his rage. Ivar shrugged him off, his face a bloody pulp, and the two enemies rolled away from each other.

Hundr scrabbled in the bilge for a weapon and came up with a broken arrow tip. Ivar came up with an axe, and he swung it at Hundr. The blade slammed into Hundr's Brynjar, and he gasped as pain exploded in his chest. Hundr lashed out with the broken arrow, and it stabbed into Ivar's blue eye. Ivar froze. The strength seeped out of him and Hundr yanked the arrow free and plunged its tip into his enemy's throat. Ivar the Boneless fell to his knees, black blood gurgling from the wound and his mouth moving silently as he died.

Hundr watched the son of Ragnar choking on the blood-soaked deck. The pain in Hundr's chest burned and sapped his energy, but he dropped to his knees and reached for the axe Ivar had hit him with. Hundr clenched the axe into Ivar's right hand and closed his fingers around it.

"Save a place for me in Valhalla, we will drink there together and talk of our hatred and our battles," Hundr whispered, for even though Ivar had been his great enemy, such a great champion deserved his place in Odin's Hall and his enemy's brown eye blinked in recognition. Then Ivar the Boneless, son of Ragnar Lothbrok, died there on the river Liffey. The pain in Hundr's chest pulsed and ached, and he lay down next to his great foe. He closed his eyes, welcoming the peace as the surrounding noise dwindled into the darkness.

TWENTY EIGHT

Hundr leaned against Windspear's mast, and a cool light sea drizzle spotted his face and hair. The salty spray was welcome and soothing on his swollen and bruised face. The warship he had taken from Ivar was huge, long, and deadly. Hundr glanced up at iron-grey clouds, clearing ahead into bright patches of clear sky, shining bright columns of sunlight onto the undulating grey-green swell ahead. His chest pulsed with pain where Ivar's axe had struck. Luckily, Hundr's mail had stopped the blow from cleaving his chest open, but the bruising and swelling went deep and made his breathing wheezy and rasping. Ivar was dead, but it left Hundr with only a hollow feeling, not the sense of elation or victory he had hoped his enemy's death would bring. He sailed away from Saoirse, locked away somewhere behind Dublin's walls and heavy with Ivar's child. Hundr wondered what would become of her now that her husband was dead. Ivar's son would be the ruler of his lands in Ireland now and would still need peace with Saoirse's people if he was to hold on to his father's lands. Hundr still loved her. Her pretty face would appear before his closed eye morning and night and whenever he was alone with his thoughts. Hundr knew he would never see her again. That chapter of his life was over now that Ivar was dead. There was no one left to hunt him unless Ivar's son came looking for vengeance. Hundr was free to forge his own path and make his own way, free of the horror and pain of the Northumbrian war.

"Do you trust them?" asked Sten, coming to stand with Hundr at the mast and nodding back towards the crew.

"They have sworn their oath to me, and they saw me kill Ivar." Hundr shrugged, wincing at the pain it caused. He had lost consciousness after the fight with Ivar, but he hadn't been out for long, and when he awoke, Sten was standing over the kneeling survivors of Ivar's crew, shouting and waving Warbringer above their heads. Sten had given them a choice. They could die there, with their throats cut and dropped into the Liffey's icy embrace, or they could swear an oath to serve the man with a dog's name, the Ivarsbane. Their Lord, Ivar, was dead, and so they were free to swear that oath if they wished. And so they had- each man kneeled before Hundr and kissed his sword blade. Hundr was now the commander of three ships' crews who raced East-wards under taut sails away from the Irish coast. One of those ships, the Wave Bear, he would re-turn to Haesten with her crew. That crew had lost almost half her number in the fight with Ivar's men, and they had lost brave Rollo.

"You have what you have always wanted now, lad."

Hundr looked up at the huge silver-haired war-rior, "What's that?"

"Reputation. Men will know of you wherever Northmen sail as the killer of Ivar the Boneless, Champion of the North. Suppose that makes you the champion now."

Hundr looked out to sea again, unsure what that even meant. To call oneself Champion of the North invited challenge, goaded warriors hun-gry to build their own reputation to seek you out and to try their mettle. "Doesn't seem like much," he said, thinking of the faces of those friends who had died for his reputation. Blink, Hrist, Rollo, too many dead faces.

"When I first met you, that was all you talked about, glory, reputation, fighting."

"I was a boy then. With a head full of dreams, children's dreams."

"Well, lad, you ain't a boy no longer."

Which Hundr supposed was true. He was a Sea

Commander now, a Viking leader of two crews and two Drakkar Warships. Hundr was scarred and wounded and a veteran of battles and sieges in three different countries. He was, he supposed, a warrior of reputation and a man to be feared.

"Do you still miss her? Ralla?" Hundr asked.

"Every hour of every day. She was everything to me, and I broke my oath to her, my oath of peace. I'll never see her again. I'll never go to her heaven."

"You broke that oath for me. I know it. You and the others came for me to save me from Hakon Ivarsson. I know now that you did what you did in Northumbria to save my life and the lives of the others. You gave up everything for us. You will go to Odin's Hall, where you belong."

"I belong with her, and that can never be." Sten's pale eyes glazed over, and he chewed at the patch of beard below his bottom lip. "Why did you give Ivar the blade at the end when your hate for him burned strong?" said Sten, changing the subject.

"Even though we hated each other and had taken much from one another, Ivar was what our gods want us to be. He was a Viking, a drengr. Brave, daring, a peerless fighter, and a leader. He will be welcome in Odin's Hall. Odin will need his sword on the day of Ragnarök."

Sten sighed and nodded slowly. "So, Wessex."

"Wessex." Hundr looked across the Windspear's deck. Einar sat with Hildr, tending to her wounded thigh. Einar had regained his famous ferocity in the battle of the Liffey. He had fought and turned the tide in the push against Ivar's Irishmen. *Einar might think he wants to settle down with Hildr and live a peaceful life, but there is no peace for men like us. We are drengr. We choose the life on the Whale Road. We hunt and fight for glory, reputation, and silver. There is no settling down.* Ragnhild huddled close with Kolo. She bathed and wrapped his wounds, and they spoke softly to each other.

"What will we do once you have returned Haesten's ship to him?"

"We'll give Haesten back the Wave Bear and his men. Help him fight his war against the rich King of Wessex. Then, if Ragnhild wants to go to Upsala, we will take her. Then we do what we were born to do, we sail the seas, and we fight whether we go east, south, north or west. We take our warships and our blades and show the gods our courage."

BOOKS IN THIS SERIES

The Viking Blood and Blade Saga

Viking Blood and Blade
(The Viking Blood and Blade Saga Book 1)
865 AD.

The fierce Vikings stormed onto Saxon soil hungry for spoils, conquest, and vengeance for the death of Ragnar Lothbrok.

Hundr, a Northman with a dog's name... a crew of battle hardened warriors... and Ivar the Boneless.

Amidst the invasion of Saxon England by the sons of Ragnar Lothbrok, Hundr joins a crew of Viking warriors under the command of Einar the Brawler. Hundr fights to forge a warriors reputation under the glare of Ivar and his equally fearsome brothers, but to do that he must battle the Saxons and treachery from within the Viking army itself...

Hundr must navigate the invasion, survive brutal attacks, and find his place in the vicious world of the Vikings in this fast paced adventure with memorable characters.

Viking Blood And Blade

Axes For Valhalla (Book 3 In The Viking Blood And Blade Saga)

866 AD.

Saxon England burns under attack from the Great Heathen Army. Vicious Viking adventurers land on the coast of Frankia hungry for spoils, conquest and glory. Hundr and the crew of the warship Seaworm are hunted by Ivar the Boneless, a pitiless warrior of incomparable fury and weapon skill.

Amidst the invasion of Brittany and war with the Franks, Hundr allies with the armies of Haesten and Bjorn Ironside, two of the greatest warriors of the Viking Age. Ivar the Boneless hunts Hundr, desperate to avenge the death of his son at Hundr's hand. To survive, Hundr must battle against fearsome Lords of Frankia, navigate treachery within the Viking Army itself, and become a warrior of reputation in his own right.

Hundr must navigate the war, survive Ivar's brutal attacks, and find his place in the vicious world of the Vikings in this unputdownable, fast paced adventure with memorable characters.

ABOUT THE AUTHOR

Peter Gibbons

Peter is an author from Warrington in the United Kingdom, now living in County Kildare, Ireland. Peter is a married father of three children, with a burning passion for history.

Peter grew up enjoying the novels of Bernard Cornwell and David Gemmell, and then the historical texts of Arrian, Xenophon, and Josephus. Peter was inspired by tales of knights, legends and heroes, and from reading the tales of Sharpe, Uhtred, Druss, Achilles, and Alexander, Peter developed a love for history and its heroes.

For news on upcoming releases visit Peter's website at www.petermgibbons.com

THE WRATH
OF IVAR

*The Viking Blood and
Blade Saga (Book 2)*

By Peter Gibbons

Made in the USA
Middletown, DE
15 October 2023

40808900R00210